The voice of my soul

by

RICHARD E. PEARSON

What's going on??!!!

Fuck! How did I get myself in this situation?! I can not believe this! If I scream, or struggle much more than I am, Nanna is going to come out here, find this asshole trying to force his penis inside me, and probably have a heart attack. And if I don't do anything, he's going to be knee deep inside me in about three seconds.

How do I just keep attracting idiots! I can't believe he's actually trying to do this!! To think I used to think that his not taking no for an answer was sexy. I thought it was just him being confident. Shit! All of my friends and that little voice inside me, said leave him the hell alone and I should have listened. Now here I am on the verge of tears, about to be raped in the foyer of my own grandmother's house and there's nothing I can do about it.

No, fuck that! Who does he think he is, coming up in my house thinking he's gon' do whatever the fuck he wants...like he's just going to have his way with me whether I like it or not. I don't think so!!! I promised myself a long time ago that this shit would never happen to me again, and it's not; at least not today!

O.K., O.K., O.K., baby..., wait..., wait..., baby..., wait. Slow down...slow down. I'm not ready for you yet. I'm not ready for you, baby...wait...please...wait. Can you just get me ready first, baby? Please, baby. You know how I like it. Oh yes, baby that's it...yeah, kiss me there...oh, yes baby yes. Oh, yes...yes that's it...ummm, that feels so good...baby, ooooh...Ok...baby...we've got to stop, before we wake up Nanna...now let me do you back.

All I could think was' God please don't let Nanna have moved those vice grips from behind the umbrella stand'. And,' please let me be able to get my hand over his mouth in time so Nanna doesn't hear him scream'.

Oh, baby...mmm...yeees...does that feel good ...yeah?.. Well...how about this!!!" My prayers were answered as my left hand covered Brent's mouth, just as he let out an involuntary wince. "...how does this feel, you slimy little bastard! Now, back the fuck up before I rip your nuts off! And I suggest that you be real slow and easy, cause if you make any sudden moves, I'm gon' get to twistin' and workin' out like I was Jackie Wilson and Chubby Checker's lil' baby sis all rolled into one up in here, and if you think your shit hurts now, well you ain't seen jack. Now first of all, did you not hear me when I told you, that I no longer want to see your trifflin' married ass? I mean, you...you didn't seem to hear that. Or maybe you just thought that that was the cue for you to have your way with me, against my will. Hmmm...is that it? Did you think I just wanted you to talk me into being fucked, even after I begged and pleaded with your ignorant ass to stop? Is that what you thought I meant??? Well...tell me something Brent, do you feel like being talked into anything right now?! Excuse me??!! I couldn't hear you!!!

Well look, I'm gon' to make this real short and sweet, 'cause you don't seem to grasp complicated concepts and, well...you know, now that I have your attention and all, I just feel the need to re-cap. Basically, our shit is over and I don't want your sorry ass in my house anymore. OK? I...don't...want...you...anymore! Is that plain enough for you? You lied to me about Rachael and you must have smooth forgotten all about your *wife,* 'cause the chick's name never even came up. And for the record,

3

when I say "stay the fuck away from me" that means don't call me, don't write me, don't even think about approaching me anymore, ever again! There is no equivocation here. That's all she wrote…point blank, end of story. Do you understand?!! Are we clear about that?!!!..what?!!! I suggest you speak up, before I really start puttin' a grip on your shit. Now, let's try this one mo' 'gin, shall we? I know you know that Nanna is very sickly, cause I just told you that, so you're not going to make a lot of noise on your way out, right? Nod yes, like a good boy... Good boy!! Yes. Yes! Very nice. You see, you can understand English. And now that you know how it feels to be touched in a way that makes you uncomfortable and makes you feel really, really vulnerable, not to mention a great deal of pain, why don't you just remember that in case you get the idea to do somebody else like this, 'kay. Oh, and one more thing, just so there's no further misunderstanding between us, if you ever get any ideas about some kind of revenge or if it should ever happen that you try to *fuck* me again, literally or figuratively, you will wish to God you had never met me! And I guaran-damn-tee you it will be such slow and painful torture, that it'll make this shit look like a fucking walk in the park. We clear??!! Good! Now get your punk ass the fuck up out of my house, bitch!!!

I had made sure that Brent was more than half way out of the door before I released the grip on the vice that had securely locked around his genitals and in my haste to get back inside, I slammed the door a little harder that I had planned. As Brent limped off, I listened to him spew vulgarities about my mental health. My mind was racing and the only thoughts that I could clearly focus on was 'Oh,

4

God! What just happened here? What if Nanna would have walked in? What if I wasn't fast enough to get the vice? What if he saw what I was trying to do before I could...? Oh God, how did I get to this point in my life?' *Nanna's voice snapped me out of my thoughts before I could get to deep.* "Baby, you alright out there, I heard a noise?" *Through sheer determination I was able to clear my head and respond,* "Oh, uh...no Nanna, everything is fine. That was Brent, he just left and he um...accidentally slammed the door".

"Oh, ok, I'm going to bed now then chile'. Don't forget to lock up, ok?"

"I won't Nanna"

"Ok. Nite nite baby"

"Nite nite Nanna. I love you."

I hadn't realized how afraid I was at the time, but as I locked the door to the foyer, I noticed that my hand was trembling. I really needed to talk to somebody. I didn't exactly know what I wanted to say, but I needed to hear a friendly voice and to have someone just be there with me for a minute 'til I could really clear my head.

"Hello, is Rennie there?"

"Speaking."

"Hey, girl it's Shay. What you doin'?

"Nothing, I was getting ready for bed. Why what's up?"

"Nothing, I just needed somebody to talk to".

"You sure you're alright, sweetie?...honey what's wrong? Why are you crying?"

"Brent just left, here and he tried to force himself on me.

"He did what?!!! Are you O.K., do you need to go to the hospital? Do you want me to come over...?"

"No, no I'm fine. I just need somebody to talk to. He

didn't do it and I made sure that he'll think about it before he tries to do that shit to anybody else. Nanna keeps a pair of vice grips behind the umbrella stand and luckily I was able to get to them...so basically I let him know I'd fuck his shit up, real bad if he ever tried something like that with me again. The bad part is that I still have to work with him for the rest of my rotation at the hospital."

"Look Shay, I'ma tell you like this because you my girl and I love you. You know, I know Keith hurt you a lot and that you're still trying to get over that, but the last five guys that you've dated have been married or crazy. I know you just found that out about Brent, but you knew about Don, Chris, James, Jean and Thoroun before you started messin' with them. Girl, I love you, but you've got to stop dealing with motherfuckers like that. I mean, c'mon now, you didn't know he was married at first, I'll give you that, but you did know was crazier than a fucking loon after he pulled a gun on that guy that he thought was tryin' to talk to you. And that was only two weeks after you started messin' with him. I mean, Shay you're not some ghetto babe. You're educated and you've got a lot going for yourself...baby, you've just got to stop getting involved with these nutty motherfuckers."

"Rennie, you think I don't know all that. That's the only reason why he was here tonight in the first place, so I could tell him that we were finished. I swear you pick the wrong times to get overprotective. I just needed you to listen to what I had to say and just be there with me, without being judgmental...without...look, I gotta go. I'll talk to you later. Kiss Rashan for me".

"...Shay, wait...I...I'm..."

"Bye Rennie."

I hate when she gets all pious and shit. Like she's never dated anybody who wasn't exactly right for her. That's part of the reason why I kept dating Brent, even when I realized he was a little off. Rennie was right there with that "girl, you need to drop him" shit and I got rebellious. It was a stupid move and I realize that, but I thought I could handle it. I mean, he was a little strange and somewhat overbearing at times, but he was very sensitive most of the time, and really seemed to understand a lot of the things that I had never told anyone else. And besides, at twenty-six years old, truthfully I've had sex with probably over 100 different guys, but Brent is the only one that I ever had an orgasm with. Don't get me wrong, I am not a hoe. It's just that I haven't always found it easy to find a place where I fit in. I mean, outside of my family, and sometimes even with them, I've had a hard time finding a place where I feel safe and secure and where I can be me and not have people say I was acting too white, too black, too preppy, too ghetto, too whatever. Growing up, my black friends couldn't understand why I liked archery and Guns & Roses, and my white friends didn't understand my unconditional love for Public Enemy or how I could possibly even listen to anything Farrakhan had to say (even though I'm not a Muslim). I never really fit in completely anywhere. And, in my defense, when it comes to all the guys I've been with, well let's just say I've been diligent in the pursuit of my happy place. I've come close to finding it with two or three guys, but overall I haven't had much success.

Initially I thought I had found my niche with Brent. But it was just sex. Incredible, mind-blowing sex, but just sex nonetheless. See the thing was that it wasn't like it was a fluke with him. I mean, I came and came and

7

came...every time we had sex. It got to the point where I thought I had some kind of problem. Like maybe I was a nymphomaniac, 'cause I just couldn't stop thinking about gettin' it in. That's all I ever wanted to do. I was addicted to orgasms. And, while I know that you can't build a relationship around orgasms, let me tell you, they do go a long way toward laying the foundation of an emotional comfort zone. Either that or my body just felt so good that my mind said 'damn a comfort zone, just keep do what you're doing'. Whatever it was, I was hooked and I had to have it. Shoot, I mean, there were even times when I was busy with stuff for work and didn't want to have sex initially, but by the time we'd finished I had cum at least four or five times. In fairness, I've always been a very sensual person, but when I was introduced to orgasms, that just put it way over the top.

I do remember feeling a little like this before when I was younger. It was a lot different of course, I mean, I didn't have orgasms then, but I still wanted sex all the time. And like I said, I just thought there was something wrong with me.

I do know that part of my feeling like there was something was wrong with me, was a direct result from the time when I was fourteen and I was raped by my brother's best friend, Tyrone. He was 19 and he had come by to see my brother, Tom, one day. We were alone for about a half hour, cause my brother and my dad had gone to run an errand. I never told anybody because I was embarrassed and I guess in part, because I didn't really think they'd believe me anyway. I didn't think they'd believe me because everybody knew I had had a crush on Tyrone anyway. It was just common knowledge. I mean, I got all doe eyed when he came around and contrary to almost everybody else's experience of me in my early teen years, I was sweet as pie when it came to Tyrone. I had it bad for him and my body responded to him in ways that I wasn't entirely comfortable with. I mean, crush or no crush, I was only fourteen and mentally I just was not ready to have sex. And even though I had often imagined kissing and holding (and maybe even grinding on him), I had only ever imagined what sex might be like a few times. It was just too scary and I couldn't even relax enough to fantasize properly. I mean, I could get pregnant or an STD or whatever.

But that day, while he was waiting for my brother to get back, I sensed something was different. Because, before when I laughed too hard at his stupid jokes or batted my eyes at him, he didn't really even seem to notice. When I think about it now, I know that that was because my brother had always been there with us, every time before this one. But this time it was just him and I, and he was paying attention to me. This time he was laughing at my stupid jokes! So, when he admired my ring, I blurted out that he could hold it if he wanted to, and almost immediately wished I hadn't. It just seemed like such a stupid, kid thing to say. Never mind that I was a kid, I was doing my damnedest to impress him with how mature I was. And I was, if I say so myself, mature for my age. As I've said, I wasn't interested in a lot of the typical things that little black girls did, like double dutch or learning steps (don't get me wrong I could hang with the best of them, but it just wasn't enough to hold my interest for very long). I was more interested in things like horseback ridding, kayaking, and archery (which weren't exactly easy to find in North Philadelphia in the early 80's). And of course

9

those things conferred a certain level of maturity onto me, or so my fourteen year old reasoning went. In any event, I momentarily thought I'd blown any chance of impressing Tyrone, cause he had stopped talking and was just looking at my mouth with this goofy look on his face. I didn't know what the look meant or how I should take it so I just kept talking.

When he kissed me, I nearly swooned at first. I felt all excited and though I tried to calm myself down and at least control my physical reaction to him, it was too late. It was like my body had a mind of it's own at that point. I remember feeling some kind of embarrassed that my nipples were hardening and there was nothing I could do to stop them. I just knew he'd be able to see them through my blouse, if we ever stopped kissing. Not that I wanted that to happen.

It was when I began to feel the moisture between my legs that I knew we had to stop. I had never felt anything like this before. I didn't want to stop, but aroused or not, and I was highly aroused, I was too scared to go any further.

That's where the problem came. We'd been kissing for what seemed like a heavenly hour or so, but was really only about five minutes. When I said I wanted to stop, he initially told me we wouldn't do anything that I didn't want to do. I could see his eye's dip momentarily as he spoke and when he smiled, I was mortified that my nipples were just not listening to my brain telling them to stop sticking out like that. Anyway, we went back to kissing. But two minutes later he put his hand under my skirt and, before I had a chance to protest, he felt the wetness that had soaked through to my panties. I snatched his hand away, but he called me a tease, held me down by my wrists, and forced

10

himself inside me.

I remember that anger and astonishment were the overriding emotions that I felt. He must have been out of his fucking mind! I'd said stop, told him I wasn't ready to do this, told him that I was a virgin and that I wasn't ready to have sex and that I wanted the first time to be special, but he just kept doing what he wanted to do anyway. And what was worse, was that it hurt! So not only was my first time not going to be special, it wasn't even going to be something that I wanted; and it hurt!! I was absolutely livid! How could he have had the nerve to do this to me when I had told him I didn't want to have sex, especially when he knew that my father, my brother, my cousins and basically my whole family would all take turns beating his ass, in shifts around the clock, if they saw what he was doing to me, even if I had consented to it. Not to mention, that I hadn't consented, and it didn't even feel good. No, scratch that, it fucking hurt!!!

After he was done he rolled off of me and started fixing his clothes, as I lay there stunned, trying to figure out what had just happened. When he saw that I was just laying there he said "you better get your clothes on. Tom and your father'll probably to be back any second".

As I started to make a comment, I heard my dad's car pull up. I jumped up and pulled my panties back on and as I did I noticed that he was still wearing the ring that I said he could hold, before this little stunt of his. I was still furious and the thought that he was about to take something else of mine made me lose it. My blood was boiling and just as Tyrone began walking toward Tom, who was walking through the door with my father in toe, I smashed my mom's favorite imitation crystal lamp over his head. He fell to the floor with a pathetic howl. It seemed like blood just starting gushing from the wound in the back left side of his head near his temple. Tom stood stark still in shock, causing my father to run into his back.

After the initial shock wore off, they rushed Tyrone to the hospital. My mom had just gotten home as they were ready to leave for the emergency room and stayed behind with me. After they left for the hospital my mom asked me what happened. I told her the same thing that I had told Tom and my dad, which was that Tyrone took something that was mine and wouldn't give it back, which was technically true. My family members were all rather shocked because even though they knew that I had a sharp tongue, I rarely ever tried to back it up with actions. Ultimately, they knew that it would take a lot to get the kind of rise out of me that Tyrone got. I was of course put on punishment and my dad half-heatedly lectured about the merits of turning the other cheek and being a young lady. No one ever questioned me further about the incident and I never saw Tyrone around the house again. I know everyone in my family believed that there was more to the story than I had let on, but I never told anyone the true story.

At the moment I smashed the lamp, I decided that I would never be violated like I'd been by Tyrone ever again; and that if I ever was, it would be over my dead body.

The ironic thing is that it was because of that experience that I began to have sex voraciously. About two months after Tyrone had received thirty-two stitches, courtesy of yours true, I began to think about the things that led up to the rape. I remembered the excitement I felt initially; the shortness of breath, the stirring in my groin, the hardness of my nipples, the wetness that had completely drenched my panties, and the involuntary tremors I felt when he kissed my neck, and it was at that point that I

12

began to masturbate...a lot.

But even though my newfound pastime felt good and was somewhat satisfying, it wasn't quite the same kind of experience as having someone else touch me. So, when I turned fifteen, I had my first consensual sexual experience. It was really awkward and pretty much over before it really started (all four times). From that point on I have always tried to achieve the kind of pleasure I got just before Tyrone violated my innocence, but I never could...until Brent. I had damn near given up on the idea that I would ever be that stimulated again, primarily because I had convinced my self that I had built the whole thing up in my mind. And to some extent, I guess that that's true. I think that part of the thrill of being with Tyrone (and probably Brent to), before it got out of hand, was that there was a hint of danger. I had no intention of going all the way, but still there was an eminent fear of being caught by my family members, the thought that someone would walk in any minute or that Tyrone might even discuss us kissing or grinding with my friends or one of my family members.

But in any event, I'd never really felt at home with a man, after Tyrone, and I'd come to expect that distance to be there and like I said, I just chalked it up to there being something wrong with me. I did come to get used to the distance I felt in relationships and I had even convinced myself that I liked the distance, that it somehow made me stronger. I mean, because of it, I knew where I stood and what I could expect from a man. I never let them get close enough to hurt me in any real way, especially not mentally. Of course, I slipped up once with the Keith that Rennie was talking about. I fell for his sincerity. He was just so damn sweet and unassuming in the beginning that I was taken in by his game.

Unfortunately, the bastard turned out to be a lazy, shiftless, un-ambitious, underachieving slug, with absolutely no plan for the future. Not that I'm bitter or anything, but what's worse is that it took me four years to find out who the real Keith was. I had put just about everything I had into making things work with him, but he just wouldn't or couldn't commit to putting in the same effort to make our relationship work. I mean, we were engaged, living together and I was just starting nursing school full time and working two part time jobs, and he had this one bullshit little rinky-dink gig in a women's clothing store and for him, that was it. He wasn't making any real effort to finish the four courses he needed to complete his degree in education, and he had no plans on doing anything other than what he was doing at that moment.

I will say that he enjoyed the work and was pretty good at getting the women to buy things. But when I asked him to get another job to help out with the finances and so that we could start saving a little for our future, he started talking that space shit that men are always talking about, and about how scary the idea of marriage was to him. Now granted, I probably could have found a different way to put it, when I asked him if the idea of being ass-out on the street was as "scary", but I was not in the mind frame to be emphasizing at that point. The bottom line was that we needed more money to make ends meet (or even have them effectively wave at each other, for that matter) and he just refused to do anything about it at all.

Well, whatever. To make a long story short, he couldn't handle it. He broke off the engagement and moved back to Arizona with his father and stepmother. At that point I got rid of the apartment and moved in with my mom's mother. I get so mad when I think about what a

14

disappointment he turned out to be. We really could have had something special, if he would've had just that much more ambition, the sniveling little... OK maybe I am a little bitter.

Be that as it may, after my Keith experience I was definitely not going to let anybody else in for a long while (literally or figuratively). There was just too much potential to be hurt. Unfortunately, even though I was resolved on a mental level, I still had needs to be dealt with on the physical level. So, I started to date the safest men I knew, married ones. I know what you're thinking, but I'm not a home-wrecker. It's just that my sensual side, unfortunately didn't just disappear when I decided to close up the emotional side of me. In my defense, I should say that I never approached these men and I never tried to get them to leave their wives. I wasn't interested in that. They were only there for one reason, which was to satisfy my momentary desire for companionship. There was no need to commit to anything and there was no possible emotional attachment, because the distance factor was inherent in these relationships. I didn't have a man; I just had 'friends' that I could be with whenever I wanted. I could have my fun and not have to be bothered about whinny momma's boys wanting to sleep over or wanting to spend more time with me or getting jealous about the number of male friends I have. It was perfect. And above all, there was no need for me to lie to them and they didn't need to lie to me. That's always been my Achilles heal. I can abide a lot of things, but I won't be lied to. Life is too short to have to play games with a man I'm sleeping with.

As fate would have it, I had to stop sleeping with married men, though, because one day one of my 'friend's' wives called me. She said she had found my number in the

15

back of her husband's wallet and that she suspected that her husband was running around on her and that she just wanted meet with me. I was intrigued by her request to meet me and impressed by her boldness in asking, so I agreed to meet with her. She was a tall, very attractive, shapely, Caramel colored woman. She looked like she worked out regularly and I couldn't figure out why any man would want to cheat on a woman who was this gorgeous. I mean, I'm no slouch, but damn! This woman could be a supermodel.

I nervously tripped when I extended my hand and as she caught me with an unexpected swiftness, I started to wonder if this meeting thing was such a good idea. This Amazon could whip my petite little ass and would have every right to do so.

"Careful sweetheart. Are you all right? I'm Rene' and you must be Shelita." Rennie went on to say that she had suspected that her husband, Thoroun, was cheating on her and that she simply wanted to hear it from my own lips, woman to woman. I'll never forget the hurt look on her face and the pain in her voice when I told her that we had indeed been sleeping together for the past seven months. It was like she knew what the answer would be, but still hoped that maybe it would be different somehow when the words left my lips.

We talked for about two hours and she told me about their seven year marriage and her husband's other suspected infidelities, her own affairs that she had recently engaged in, in response to her husband, talked about their five year old son Rashan and even discussed their eminent divorce.

I must admit that it was one of the weirdest conversations that I have ever had. But it was, on the other

16

hand, one of the most sincere and honest ones that I've had as well. Rennie and I both told Thoroun about our conversation that night and the next day, they filed for an uncontested divorce. Rennie and I however kept in touch and became really, really good friends. The strange thing was that it was because of the devastation and havoc that I had helped to wreak on Rennie's family that I decided to drop all of my married friends and to really gain a new kind of a respect for the institution.

Even so, I still wasn't ready to do the whole relationship vulnerability thing. So, I figured maybe I could find unattached men that were the furthest from the type that I could actually see myself settling down with. And that worked for a while. When I felt myself getting too serious, I could think of that one fatal flaw and I was usually right back to where I needed to be.

Brent's flaw was threefold. He's a security guard at my hospital, he's been in that position for the past five years and he has no plans to leave in the near future. As far as his flaw went anyway, Brent was perfect. In short, he had no ambition. He was just like Keith, in that regard. And anybody that reminded me of Keith was only going to get but so far with me. There was one big difference with Brent, though. Because even though Keith had no ambition to speak of, he was still pretty honest and wore his heart on his sleeve. Brent was kind of brooding and quiet most of the time, so even when I did think about his flaw I still felt the excitement of his dark side. The fact that he had pulled a gun on a perfect stranger for no reason, other than that he thought that the guy was flirting with me, was scary, yet strangely exciting. Don't get me wrong, I'm not some masochist, or some wanna be gangster chick. My position is and has always been that if he would ever put his hands on me, he will wish he hadn't. But for some reason I can't really explain, when he pulled the gun on that guy, I got really wet and we had the best sex of my life, that night. In fact it was the very first time I ever had an orgasm. And after that, I was hooked. It was like a drug. I couldn't stop. Until I found out that not only had he lied to me about being married, but also tried to get with my best friend, Rachel. I wouldn't have minded either one of those things, if he had just been honest with me. But he fucked up and I heard him trying to make plans with her, the day after she told me that he had done it the first time and he had denied that he would even want to talk to Rachel at all, saying that she was just too skinny and wasn't at all his type.

The thought about Rachel makes me wish I could talk to her right now. Shoot! I can't believe her. She's away on vacation in the Bahamas and if I know Rachel, she's probably got Dexter St. Jox, Knee deep in her groove right now. Rachel and I have always been each other's grounding. I've got to give it to her, she can always look past the emotionality of a situation and offer really good practical advise. Which is what I need right now. The one thing I'm sure about right now is that I've got to get away from all this stuff. I've got a practicum coming up in two weeks, I don't how I'm supposed to deal with Dickhead at work now, and I hate to admit it, but all that excitement made me horny as all hell. And seeing as how I just kicked Mr. Orgasm's sorry ass to the curb, I don't know when I'm gon' get some of the good stuff again. Well, I'm not going to think about that right now. Right now I'm going draw that hot bath I was thinking about and I'm just gon' let Calgone take me away.

Shit! A hot bath probably wouldn't be the best Idea if I'm not gon' to be thinking about sex. Ever since Dickhead showed me how to position myself under the water, I can almost have an orgasm from that alone. And every since, I've been a freak like Adina, in the bathroom.

I guess I'm going have to face it, they'll just be no more intense really explosive, dig my nails into his back, orgasms for me until I can break somebody else in and that's not even going happen until I can at least sort out some of the bullshit in my life right now. And goodness knows how long that's going to take. My Nanna's recently been diagnosed with a heart condition, I'm so sick of school I can't even begin to put it in words, I'm gonna have to see a guy who tried to force me to have sex with him, every day at work for the next two and a half months; I don't have a man or even any prospects, and I'm horny as hell.

This shouldn't be as big a problem as it is, but let's face it; I need a regular tension reliever. I've gotta say, I hate the idea of just going cold turkey. I mean, if this had been a gradual process, I could handle it better, but it's only been a few hours and I feel like a crack-head who was just told that she can't have anymore. They should develop an orgasm patch or something for people trying to quit, man.

I did have a fleeting thought that maybe I could try women for a while. I bet Rennie wouldn't mind. She started experimenting with her sexuality after Thoroun, and I gotta say she made some of her escapades sound pretty damned good. Like, she said that she once met this cute

19

little white girl named Becky who was bored with married life and wanted a change of scenery. Becky was thirty-two years old, and was a short little red head with large perky breast, a small waist, shapely legs, and to quote Rennie "an ass that would put a sister to shame".

She said that Becky licked her in places and gave her better head than any man she'd ever met. Rennie said she couldn't believe how enthusiastic and energetic the red head chick was. I remember the phone call I got after she had gotten home that night. "Girl, I have seen the Promised Land...she sucked my toes and kissed every part of my body for an hour, and then she got down to the real thing. Girl, excuse my French but, she did a thing where she tossed my salad and ate it at the same time and...I thought I was going to pass out. I really thought I knew what an orgasm felt like, but I know now I had my first real orgasm today." Rennie also said that Becky taught her how to give good head as well. To hear Rennie tell it, she's got one heck of a head game at this point...and my fleeting thought process went something like this...well head is head and as long as I didn't have to reciprocate...and her breasts didn't touch me...and she cut her hair real short or tied it up for a while.... But like I said the thought was fleeting. I'm just trippin' a little at this point. But the bottom line is that I'm a grown woman and come hail or high water, my sensuality will simply not determine who I am. I've lived without orgasms before and damn it, if I have to, I'll live without them again. Shoot, I'm an adult and I can even give them to myself now anyway. And who knows, maybe they will be as intense and hot and wonderful as the ones Dickhead gave anyway. Yeah. Yeah! That's right, I don't need a man. I don't need anybody, just a bunch of strong batteries...of course I will need to get that

20

*box of stuff out of storage in Nanna's basement...and I wish
I could talk to Rachel.*

*Oh God, I can't believe it's eleven-thirty already.
I'd better get to bed. I'm going to have a long day ahead of
me tomorrow. Maybe I'll get lucky and Dickhead won't
show up for work.*

*I had just drifted off to sleep when the phone ring.
And as I sat halfway up in bed I had that jittery feeling in
the pit of my stomach that I usually get when I'm startled
out of a sound sleep. The feeling turned mostly to irritation
though as I looked at the clock and couldn't believe
someone had the audacity to dare call me at this hour on a
work night.*

"...whoever this is calling me at three o'clock in the
morning better have a *damn* good reason!" I curtly
whispered into the phone.

"Look ho, I don't know who you think you selling wolf
tickets to, but I know your momma, so you best slow your
roll." I screamed louder than I meant to when I recognized
Rachel's voice through my grog and suddenly I didn't care
what time it was anymore.

"...Rachel, girl where are you and why are you just calling
me now, ho?! I wanted to talk to you soooo bad earlier.
Girl, Brent showed his ass when I told him it was over!!
But I'll tell you about it. First tell me about your trip."

"Well, we pulled into the Bahamas three nights ago and it
is soo pretty down here, Shay you would not believe it. I'm
sorry I haven't called until now sweetie, but, guuurl there
ain't been nothing *but* sexy chocolate down here from day
one. I mean, when we got off the plane, I had to take a cab
to the hotel and even the cab driver was fine!! I tried to
hold out as long as I could, but you know what a sucker I

21

am for a chocolate man with an accent. So when we got to the hotel, I decided to give him a ride of my own. And Shay, Shay, Shaaay lemmie tell you, I don't know what it is about island brothers, but they be swinging the real good dick, mon" Rachel half sang into the phone in a pitiful Jamaican accent.

"OOOOh, you nasty little trollop, tell me you did *not* do the cab driver, Rae Rae."

"Humph, yes I did girlfriend, repeatedly, and well, I might add!" Rachel defiantly replied.

"You are such a slut puppy, and you better tell me about every single juicy detail, too." I teased.

"Girl, put it this way, if I had to leave tonight, I could say I got my freak on enough for both of us, already. But we'll have plenty of time to talk about that later. How are you doing? What happened with Brent? Tonight was the night you were going to tell him right?"

"Do you know that *nigger* tried to force himself on me when I told him it was over!!! I wanted to beat his fucking ass so bad!! I started to call Tom and tell him about it, but you know how crazy Tom is. He would have got Danny and some of their boys and literally lynched Brent's ass. But I didn't want them getting in trouble over that little punk, so I didn't tell him. Not yet anyway. I'm going to wait to see if he tries to start some shit at work or not. "

"Oh my God, baby are you alright!? I mean, he didn't..."

"No, I stopped him with a pair of vice grips that Nanna keeps in the foyer, but he would have if I hadn't." I replied, sensing the anger well up in me again.

"Well, what you want to do? Girl you know I got your back. Say the word and I know some brothers that'll cut that motherfucker off *smooth* and nobody'll ever be the wiser. I mean, straight break him off somethin' proper

22

like." I tried not to, but I found myself laughing in spite of myself and at that moment I really appreciated having Rachel as a friend. She had a knack for making me laugh, even in the worst of times.

"...that's why you my girl Rae Rae. I always know you got my back. But naw, I'm just going to go work and go about my business. And if he don't start none, won't be none".

Rachel and I talked until about six o'clock that morning and when we got off the phone I felt like everything was going to be alright. And for the next few weeks, they actually were. Dickhead kept his distance and didn't so much as look at me right up until the day he quit about seven months later. I must say I was having some quite satisfying orgasms with my little box of toys that I had taken out of storage from Nanna's basement. Well, at least they were satisfying compared to nothing at all. Granted, I still felt empty and kind of unfulfilled inside, but being a little uncomfortable with my station in life at that point was at least a manageable problem. Well...I should say it was until I met Gerald.

What did you say your name was?

I thought I was going to have jack Nurse Tamika up that day, and I almost did. She was team leader…well, at least that was her title, and she was always trying to play little miss matchmaker. And since Kimberly and I were the only two unmarried LPN's on the floor, we caught the brunt of her messin'. Unfortunately, Kim was on vacation when Dr. Thompson started and so, that left me. Tamika tried to be slick and volunteered to show him around the unit and when she got to me she said "and this is our newest LPN, Shelita Peterson. She's the new kid on the block. We call her Shay or Miss Shay whichever you prefer. She's twenty-six, single and she lives in Brook lawn. You did say you were single too didn't you, Dr. Thompson?" I could have slapped the fool out of her for that alone, but she kept going. "Shay, maybe *you* could show Jerry around since he's new to town." I think he probably sensed an ass whipping about to commence when he spoke up and said, "uh...it's Gerald and thanks for the offer, but I wouldn't want to put Ms. Peterson on the spot like that. However, I'd be delighted if someone could show me where the cafeteria is."

I hadn't been with a man in seven months and I had to admit he was kind of cute. I had to catch myself from fantasizing about what he would be like in bed when I felt my freakin' nipples starting to become erect (*I swear they get me in more trouble*). I hoped he wouldn't notice as he stood there in front of me, so I said I'd be happy to show him where the cafe was, mostly, so we wouldn't have to stand across from each other and I could get my composure

24

back.

On the way to the cafe we joked about the look on my face when nurse Tamika said that he could call me "Shay or Ms. Shay" whichever he preferred. He said "…I could tell that didn't sit too well with you. I mean, if looks could kill, there'd be a lot of slow singing around nurse Tamika's house at this moment." We laughed and talked for about an hour and he seemed like a really nice guy. He had a good since of humor, he smelled great and he wasn't afraid to say what was on his mind. He was exactly the kind of guy that I had tried to avoid every since Keith and I wasn't ready to be vulnerable like that again.

My mind kept telling me to slow down, look for a flaw. I needed to stop thinking about sex with this man and just concentrate on finding out exactly what makes this seemingly magnificent specimen of a man, just as big a jerk as the other men that I've gone out with in the past. Or what made him, at the very least, an unsuitable candidate for a mate. I tried to find something quickly, but I couldn't. After all was said and done, I had learned was that he was 32 years old, had a gorgeous smile, he had recently moved to town from Kansas, was in his fourth year as a pediatric intern, he had been divorced for close to five years now, he had a wonderful sense of style, he loved kids and someday planned to have his own pediatric clinic. Nothing! There was absolutely nothing there to stop a mental connection from developing. Well, there was one tiny little thing. But, even it was flimsy in comparison to the positives. In the end, he seemed intelligent and physically, from what I saw, there was no major problem either. I had been celibate for the better part of a year and my hormones were finally threatening to get the best of me. I ached for intimate physical contact with a man…hell I needed it. And here I

25

could tell, I was on dangerous ground.

I had barely met this man and already I was fantasizing about what his favorite positions might be. What was worse though was that there was almost nothing that I knew about him that would stop me from forming an emotional attachment as well. He was Keith waiting to happen all over again! The unfortunate thing though was that, like so many times before, my body had a mind of its own and didn't seem to give a damn about my mind's petty little concerns at that point. And even as I heard it making plans to show Gerald around New Jersey (i.e. my bedroom), I knew that it was a mistake.

"'Shan, baby I'm not going to tell you anymore, go to bed. Don't come back out here unless you really need something, O.K.?" was the standard warning that Rennie usually issued to Rashan when it was way past his bedtime and he was getting on her nerves. Tonight was different though, it was actually ten minutes before Rashan's bedtime, but Rennie had company and wanted to put him to bed early tonight. He replied, "yes, mommy" in his *I'm being pathetic and I want some sympathy* voice and Rennie's resolve to have him in bed before nine faded. "O.K. 'Shan, you can come back out for ten minutes, but that's it. You hear?" she bluffed as he bounded out of his bedroom, down the stairs and into her lap. Rashan listened intently to his mother and her guest for the next hour, trying his best to understand what all of the spelled words were and piecing together the conversation as best he could, before sleep finally got the best of him.

Rennie apologized as she got drinks for herself and her company after she had finally put Rashan down (about an hour and a half after she said he could come down for ten more minutes).

"He has straight got you wrapped around his little finger." Rennie's guest playfully teased.

"Monica, I'm so sorry, I just don't like saying no to him every since the divorce, you know."

"No, no baby don't worry about that. I'm just kidding. Your kid should come first. He is such a sweet little boy. Right now, though, I'm interested in his momma. So why don't you slip out of those shoes and relax your feet, sugar. As a matter of fact, put them right here on my lap and I'm going to give you the best massage you have ever had."

"Careful now girl, you're gonna to spoil me. I might just want this all the time, if it's as good as you say."

"Oh it's gonna be better than that baby, this is just the beginning. When I get through with you, you're not going to want anybody else to touch that beautiful body of yours, at all." Rennie could feel herself get wet as Monica's soft hands gently massaged her feet, calves and lower thighs. "Honey, let's go up stairs."
"Oh, you liked that massage, huh?" Monica teased.
"You aw'ight" Rene' retorted as she took Monica's hand and led her up to the master bedroom.

The phone rang as Rennie and Monica collapsed naked in each other's arms. Monica whispered "let the answering machine get it" between soulful kisses. Rennie was exhausted and could feel herself drifting off to sleep, but held tighter to Monica as she tried in vain to sit up in bed. "ummm, I just want to do you again and again baby, but it's already after one and I've got to work tomorrow."
"Uh-huh, you just gon' do me and leave right?" Rene' playfully questioned.
"Now c'mon baby, you know it's not like that" Monica replied in a deep voice as they both laughed quietly so-as not to wake Rashan.
"I'm gon' take a shower first O.K.!" Monica stated as she walked toward the master bath"
"Umph, umph, umph will you look at the onion on that girl" Rennie called after her.
"Make you wanna cry don't it" Monica called back as she stopped to playfully show off her nearly perfectly round behind.

I hadn't expected to hear from Rennie at least until the next morning and was somewhat shocked to hear her voice on the other end of the phone.

"Yes???!!"

"Yes???!! Damn it's like that?" Rennie asked

"Oh, hey girlie. I'm sorry. I didn't know it was you!"

"Well Damn, who'd you think it was? Anywho, I just got your message, what's up."

"You just got my message? What were you doing when I called?"

"Getting my swerve on…if you must know, and before you even ask, yes *she* is Black." Rennie stated, answering both my questions before I had a chance to ask.

"Oh Damn, I'm sorry. I'm not interrupting am I?"

"No, she's in the shower. She's about to go home. Why what's up?

"Well, if I told you that I did Gerald, tonight that wouldn't make me a bad person or anything would it?" I asked sounding like a little girl who knew she had done something wrong, but hoped some adult would say it was alright.

"Gerald? Gerald who? Not Gerald Thompson! I know you're not talking about Dr. Gerald Thompson. Mr. freckled faced white guy Dr. Gerald Thompson, not him."

"Rennnnnnie!"

"Alright, alright, alright I won't mess with you about it. Even though you tripped about Becky the way you did..."

"That was different, Rennie. I mean, Black women have to date suitable men where they can find them. Black, White, Blue, Pink or Green it doesn't matter there just aren't enough good black men to go around, but for a Black man to date a white woman is another matter."

"Shay, whether or not you've noticed, I'm a Black woman."

"Yeah...well...look it's late, don't confuse me with the facts. I need some advice here Rennie. Do you think I

29

should see him again or what?"

"Well, was it any good?"

"Yes!!! It was great!! That's what the problem is. He's a great guy, doesn't have any baggage that I can see, he gives great head and the man can move his ass like nobody's business."

"I'm sorry what's the problem again? Oh yeah, he reminds you of Keith."

"Rennie, I didn't say that."

"Well that's what you meant. And, honey I'm not gonna try to tell you what to do one way or another, but this guy doesn't sound anything like Keith to me at all. I mean, he's White, he's got a great job, he's ambitious, he's great in bed, and so forth and so on. Shoot, it was because of the shortage of guy's like that that I had to try something different my self. Not to sway you, but if you don't want him, give me his number. I know what to do with him."

"Yeah, I guess you're right. When I think about it, he's not really like Keith at all. O.K. ...yeah, thanks for listening Rennie. I really hope I didn't disturb anything with y'all."

"I told you, you didn't. She's still in the shower. She likes to take long...hot...showers. Umph, it's getting a little warm in here and I think I'm gon' join her. So, if you don't mind, sweetie..."

"Rennie, can I ask you a personal question?"

"C'mon now, girl who you talking too? Of course, you can."

"Well, You've told me about some of the more wild episodes that you've had, but what do you typically do with a woman. You know what I mean? Cause, heterosexually speaking, you just can't always jump right out there and suck a guy's dick or flip him over and get on top, the first or second time you're with him. So what's the standard

30

thing you do with a woman? I mean, I can imagine, but I figure why not just go right to the source."

"There's only one way to find out sweetie. Are you ready for that?"

"Absolutely not…humph, Rennie, as kinky as you are, I think I'd be scared of you in bed."

"Well, baby don't be *scered'* you would have no reason to be scared at all. And I guarantee you shorty, you'd have the time or your life. You let me know when you're ready and we'll see what we can see, O.K.?"

"Rennie!"

"You know you ain't doing nothing but talking smack girl and I'm talking it with you. I know you would *never* have sex with a woman, so stop trippin'. And as far as this man goes, he's available, the sex is good, and he's got a good looking future…what more do you want? Now stop beating yourself up and enjoy him for what it's worth…and get off my phone so I can go get me some."

"Bye Rennie. Thanks for your help. Love ya."

"Love you too, babe."

When I got off the phone, I thought to myself "yeah, Rennie's right. Why shouldn't I enjoy this man?" He's got more going for him than anybody I've ever dated. He's gorgeous, generous in and out of bed, he treats me like a queen, doesn't trip about my male friends, he's ambitious, and he's sensitive. What more could I ask for. Well, there is the whole white thing, but, the way I see it, he's a man first and foremost. And yeah, he may have a little less pigment than I'm used to, but I guess I can live with that. I can't believe I had actually considered turning down his invitation for a romantic three-day weekend in the Pocono's. I mean, the first man to touch my body since

31

Dickhead, makes me cum four times in three hours and I'm thinking maybe I shouldn't go because his skin happens to be lighter than mine. I know I need a vacation now.

Trouble in Reldville

I thought the weekend of the 30th would never come, but it did and finally we were on our way. It was about a two and a half hour drive to the cabin in the Pocono's. I hadn't expected the trip to be so easy and relaxed since we had only been together for about three months at that point, but we laughed and joked practically the whole way there. I thought it was amazing how similar Gerald and my views were about a lot of things. He was almost perfect. The only two things I really didn't like about him were that he sometimes smoked when he was worried or upset about something and the effeminate way he sometimes would stand when he was deep in thought. He would put most of his weight on one leg (so his butt tooted out) and he'd bend the other leg at the knee and put that foot on top of the other one. At the same time he would wrap one of his arms around his waist, while biting one of his nails on the other hand as he cocked his head to one side or another. Now a few months ago that would have been enough to exclude him as a possible mate (or just about anything else for that matter), but the fact was that I needed this and if I had to endure trivial annoyances to get it, then I was just going to have to do that. Besides, despite my desire for it not to be the case, he had really started to grow on me.

Anyway, we got to the room at about 7:30 that Friday night and we couldn't keep our hands off each other from the door. I was kind of tired at first when we got in, but I could feel myself getting all worked up when Gerald started massaging my shoulders. He started off with a gentle slow circular motion over my neck and shoulder blades and when he felt my shoulders relax he slowly moved his hands to the front of my shoulders and down to my breasts. My nipples were hard instantly and I could feel the moisture between my legs. I felt tingly all over my body as he cupped my breasts and teased the nipple between his fore and middle fingers. And I thought I'd swoon when he started kissing my neck along the nape and down to my collarbone. If I had to pick *a spot*, that was absolutely my spot. Anyway, Gerald's kisses were soft wet fluttery little kisses that made the hairs on my neck stand on end. I had unconsciously started grinding my hips backward to meet his gyrations and by now I could feel his erection though his pants.

My panties were soaked by the time he had taken off my shirt and was slowly kissing his way down my spine. When he got to my lower back he quickly took them off and immediately started massaging my outer lips of my vagina with his fingers. As he continued traveling down my back with lingering wet kisses he whispered "damn, you've got a great ass...I can't wait to fuck it" when he got to my behind. I couldn't help falling onto the bed as I reached behind me to pull him closer to the sensitive spot that he had just hit. We both laughed for a moment before he went back to the task at hand. My body twitched involuntarily as he eagerly explored my body's every orifice. Not to be outdone, I had some exploring of my own to do. And after I had had my third mini orgasm (the kind I thought I was doing O.K. giving to myself with my toys) I flipped him over and slowly began to rip the buttons off his shirt with my teeth.

Up until this point in our relationship I had held a little back, I had staved off the desire to totally quench my sexual appetite, for fear that he may get the wrong idea about me. I mean, after all, I am a lady. But I'd made up my mind that if we had lasted long enough to make it to tonight, he was going to experience the complete and total quenching of my hunger in its entire splendor. When all the buttons on his shirt were gone, I quickly took off his pants and underwear so that nothing stood between me and the object of my affection. I began to slowly kiss his chest and stomach with the kind of kiss that starts out gently, but turns into a suck that's almost like a little bite. I thought I may have been hurting him at first when I saw the little red marks that I was leaving all over his torso, but when I looked down I could tell by the size of his growing manhood that pain was not what he was feeling. I could feel him shiver as I grabbed it and began stroking it, while I kissed all around his shaven pubic area, his thighs, and his rather large sack. "What you got in here walnuts" I teased as I began to gently suck them. He moaned louder as he gently held my head in place so that I would continue stimulating the spot I had just gone over with my tongue. When the moaning became louder I stopped stroking him and pulled back so that he wouldn't cum too fast. But when he begged me not to stop, I obliged. I took him deep into my mouth and was sure to avoid inadvertently hurting him with my teeth. I had known he was able to hold off from climaxing, but I didn't know he was as adept at it as he was. I guess he was holding back a little too. After, I had been quite affectionate with his most manly part for about another ten minutes or so; I was on the verge of lockjaw and was quite pleasantly surprised to find that he was still going strong.

I felt tiny ripples of pleasure spread throughout my body as I guided him inside me from the back as I lay on my stomach. I loved this position and I was eager to try a new trick that Rachel had told me about. She said that she'd never even thought about it before, but that her cab driver friend in Jamaica told her that if she would use the back of her thighs to grab his balls in this position, it would really increase the sensation for them both. And from the way Rae Rae raved about it, I had to try it for myself. So I went right to work and sure enough Rae Rae was absolute right. I could feel every inch of him inside me deeper than I've ever felt. At first it was kind of weird and sort of hurt a little. But it wasn't a painful kind of hurt; it was a good hurt which soon turned into nothing but pleasure. And I came harder than I ever have after about five minutes. Luckily Gerald held out for a while longer and I had a two more little orgasms and was in the process of having a third before he had his first.

I had expected him to pull out when he came, but he didn't which felt great but also worried me. We had promised each other to be monogamous after our first sexual encounter, had gone down together to be tested for AIDS about two weeks before the trip and I was on the pill, but still I felt like I'd rather be safe than sorry. Before I had a chance to say anything, though, he asked "did you come?"

"Oooh, yeah. And quite a few times I might add" I responded. And as I struggled to think of how to put what I was about to say, Gerald started kissing me down there again. I couldn't believe he was about to eat me again after he had just climaxed inside me. I would not have been able to pay most of the guys that I'd dated before to do me again after they'd come and practically all of them had even worn a condom. But here was this wonderfully freaky man oblivious to the fact that he was, in all likelihood, tasting

some of his own body fluid, doing me again. Just the thought of what he was doing made me cum again and I had to stop him cause at that point I was becoming quite sore. I fell asleep wrapped in Gerald's arms thinking "can this man be for real?" I had my answer soon enough.
Up until Sunday morning, the weekend had gone almost perfectly, aside from one minor argument. Gerald was great company and sexually I had been as liberated as I had ever been. We did things this weekend that I had only ever thought about before. This is why I couldn't believe that he was trippin' about my saying that I wasn't ready to try anal sex just yet. I mean, after all we hadn't known each other *that* long. He whined and complained about us having tried everything else, and begged and pleaded up one wall and down another but I wasn't having it. Normally, I would have just said no and had that be that, and if it bothered him that much I'd remind him of where the door was. But I knew I had fallen for him when I found myself trying to explain the reason why I didn't want to do it. I thought to myself that it was probably a cultural thing. I euphemized to him, but basically, said that even though he might be able to get a white chick to just let him fuck her in the ass after he's only known her for a few months, a sister, or one like me anyway, has to know that person, *extremely well* before I could even seriously consider something like that. He seemed to understand that and just as it started raining hard outside, we had some incredible make up sex.

After it was over I laid there with my leg draped over his body as I ran my fingers through his chest hair. The bed was under the window which was open and I could feel a slight breeze blowing through. I loved the smell of the rain and I remember laying there and thinking that I couldn't believe how well this weekend had gone up to that

37

point. I drifted off thinking *I have got to do this more often.*

       I was startled out of my sleep by a loud knocking and someone screaming "Reld..., Reld open this fucking door now!!!! I know you're in there and I know that little bitch is in there with you!!! You'd better open this motherfuckin' door Reld..." I was groggy and as I sat up in bed Gerald had already pulled on his pants and was walking toward the door. I grabbed some sweats, a t-shirt and some sneakers a put them on in the bathroom, not knowing what to expect. As I threw my sneakers on I heard Gerald saying, "Antonio, what the fuck are you doing here. How'd you find out where I was...? Look, I told you I need space...and right now I'm here with a friend. You don't just barge in here screaming for me to open the fucking door. I'll be with whoever I want to be with...we are not together anymore." I had just finished tying my shoes and stood up stark straight when I heard Gerald's last comment. What the fuck did he mean 'we're not together anymore'? When I came out of the bathroom a short pale white man with a slight build and no facial hair stood in the doorway and they both looked in my direction as I hurriedly came out of the bathroom. I was ready for anything. I had no jewelry on, my clothes were loose and I had taken the opportunity to rub some Vaseline on my face, just in case I needed to handle my business. Antonio pushed his way past Gerald and was now in the middle of the room.
"Look, Reld I don't know what you think, but 'I need some space' does not mean 'we're not together anymore. It doesn't mean 'we're through'. I don't even believe you're treating me like this Reld."

"Gerald, what's going on?" I asked politely with a tinge of concern in my voice

"This is none of your fucking business, bitch!!! So stay out of it" was the response I got from Antonio, as I looked at Gerald for some since of what was going on or at the very least some since of his impending defense of my honor, which did not come.

"What did you say???" I asked to give Gerald another chance to defend me.

"You fucking heard what I said. Keep your big assed nose out of this, you fucking whore" was the response I got this time and still nothing came from Gerald in the way of defending my honor. And if that wasn't bad enough, Antonio continued "So what did she do, let you fuck *her* in the ass, Reld. Is that what changed your mind about us. For God's sake Reld, you know how they are."

"Reld???!..." I asked nastily, fed up with this ignorant little man's intrusion and insults. "Who the fuck is..." I continued, and was interrupted with

"YES, RELD, BITCH!!! AS IN GE-RALD, O.K.!! YOU LITTLE FUCKING HOME WRECKING TRAMP!!! YOU'RE ALL ALIKE! HALF THE TIME DON'T EVEN KNOW WHO THE FUCK YOU'RE FUCKING!!!" He yelled at the top of his voice.

"You know what Twon, or Toni or whatever-the-fuck your name is, you've got one more time to call me a bitch, tramp, insult me or scream at me like that and I'ma dig deep in that ass". I stepped up and admonished him, with my forefinger an inch from his head, over his protestations that I didn't scare him. I then turned again to Gerald and asked what was going on, one last time.

"Gerald, Who the fuck is this!!" I demanded through clinched teeth. I hadn't meant to scare Gerald and before that moment I didn't think I could if I wanted to. But as he stood there in that effeminate little stance of his that I hated, I could tell he was terrified.

"He...uh...was a...um...a friend of mine...you know...a while back we, um..." He stammered through a half assed explanation, only to be interrupted by Antonio.

"A while back??!! A while back??!! What the fuck do you mean a while back??!! Two months ago is not a while back, Reld. What the fuck is going on here? You were supposed to be taking some time to figure out how you felt about me. What about that Reld??!! What about our plans??!! I mean, I don't believe you're just gonna give up on what we had for some little nigger bitch cunt???!!!!!

It seemed almost like I had stepped out of my body as I watched my right fist slam into Antonio's nose and the blood begin to gush down his face. At that moment every slight that I had ever endured flashed before me. It went from Tyrone to Keith to Brent and finally to "Reld" who was now among the short list of people for whom I had let my guard down, had fallen and who had in turn betrayed me. I was outraged and as Antonio threw both his hands over his nose, I caught him with a right upper cut which knocked him flat on his back. I was busy cursing, kicking and stomping for all I was worth when Gerald finally pulled me back, which gave Antonio a chance to scamper out of the cabin, whimpering like a wounded animal.

Gerald was screaming "Shay, please stop!! Stop, calm down, you're hurting him!!" as he pulled me away from Antonio. And after the little rat bastard had left, I jerked free of Gerald's grip with a violent motion that almost surprised me. "Get the fuck off me!!! Tell me that you're not gay Gerald...tell me!! I SAID TELL ME!!" I demanded damned near at the top of my lungs.

Unanswered, I continued "Cause I don't even believe that you would have the audacity to be screwing anyone else, let alone a man, while we were still seeing each other. What the fuck were you thinking!!! You know that AIDS in rampant in the gay community! How could you put me at risk like that? How?!!! What the fuck were you thinking Gerald?" I couldn't believe what was happening and I felt sick and wanted very much to just collapse into a ball and have a good cry. But I was also furious at Gerald and couldn't bring myself to do that in front of him. "Gerald, say something!! Say any fucking thing!! But don't just keep standing there with that tired-assed look on your face" I shouted at him in frustration. As the tears started to roll down his face, Gerald began an explanation.

"Shay, I'm so sorry. I really didn't mean for this to happen. I was so confused when I met you that...well just before we met, I had been separated for years, but my divorce had just actually gone through and I had really started to question whether I could love anybody else again or even if I wanted to try. I wasn't even sure if I liked women any more and then I met Antonio. I never meant for it to happen and we only had sex a few times. And we did use condoms every time. But that's when he started talking about us becoming life partners or getting married and it just didn't feel right. So, I told him I needed some space, so I could figure out what I wanted to do. But that's when I met you and from the first moment I saw you I knew I wanted to be with you. You were so feisty and lively and so beautiful. The world seemed alright again and I knew I loved you from that moment. And I've not had sex with anybody else since you and I got together." As I listened to Gerald talk I realized that I hadn't really wanted or needed for him to say anything, because there

41

was really nothing left say. He had betrayed my trust, had lied to me, manipulated me, and put me at risk for God knows what kind of S.T.D... . I listened to him ramble as best I could until I finally had to speak up.

"Love!!! Love??!! You knew you loved me from that moment??!! Gerald that is the biggest crock of bullshit I've ever heard!!! You don't love me!!! Because if you did, you would have at least had the damned common courtesy to explain your homosexual tendencies to me from the door, so that I could make an informed decision as to whether or not I want to be with somebody who also sleeps *with men*."

"I'm not gay, Shelita…"

"What the fuck!!! You're a man who sleeps with men, that's the very fucking definition of a gay man!!! You *Asshole*!!! I can not fucking believe this…and then you have the nerve to talk about how much you love me. Please!!! You don't love me; and you weren't thinking about anybody but your damned self all along...I'm going home now and when I get back to work, I'm going to put in a request to be transferred to St. Christopher's as soon as possible. This is it Gerald!!! I don't ever want to hear from you again!!! You have to be absolutely out of your mind! Leave me the fuck alone!! I don't have shit else to say to you Gerald! I just don't fucking believe you!"

I was in the middle of cursing and packing when I heard a commotion in the living room again. "dtep adide Gerald dis is a police madder dow!" When I heard the effeminate voice, I went to investigate. As I emerged from the bedroom I found Antonio with a crimson stained handkerchief pressed to his nose and two police officers in toe, as he pointed in my direction with his free hand. "dat's her!!! das's da fucking lunatic!!! I dink' dhe broke by fucking dose!!! I want her arrested!!! I want her dhrown under da fucking jail!!!"

The cops wore thin leather jackets and thick black boots and I gathered they were state troopers. One was Black, one white and they both looked to be in about their thirties. The black one stepped forward, flashed me his badge and began speaking.

"Mam, my name is Officer Jones. This man says that you assaulted him. Is that true?"

"Wha' da fuck do you mean is id drue??? Of course id's drue!!! Don't you dee my fucking dose??? Don't you dee all the blood?? Just arres the liddle bitch!!!" Antonio interrupted and then hid behind the white officer after he had said the word "bitch".

"Sir, I'm talking to the lady right now and I'm going to have to ask you to be quite!" Officer Jones continued. "As I was saying mam, did you hit this man in the nose?"

"Yes, I did" I spoke up brazenly and perhaps a little foolishly as well. "After he pounded on our door screaming at the top of his lungs to be let in and then started calling me all kinds of *niggers* and *bitches*. I asked him to talk to me respectfully, he called me a *cunt*, and I took it to his ass!! And I'd do it again."

"Dee!! Dee!! Are you 'appy dow??!! 'aul 'er ass off to jail, dow please!!...Well, wha da 'ell are you waiting for?" Antonio demanded unable to clearly articulate the letters H, N or T.

"Jack please take Mr. Brewin outside, so he can calm himself down. I need to speak with these two for a minute." Officer Jones asked Gerald for his version of the incident after Antonio was out of the room.

"Basically, everything happened just as she said officer." Gerald said after having explained the incident in detail to

43

office Jones, between puffs of a rather nasty smelling cloved cigarette all while standing in that fucking stance of his.

"Look, Mr. Brewin seems rather upset right now and he says he wants to press charges against you, mam. So I'm going to have to take you in, but I do understand your plight. I mean, just between us he does seem a bit irrational. I have some friends at the precinct and I'll try to get your bail set as low and as quickly as possible, alright? I won't have to cuff you and we'll make it as painless as possible. But I'm gonna need you to come with me." He gave me a warm half smile as he politely gestured toward the squad car. I wanted to protest, but I was spent. It had taken all I had not to punch Gerald in the nose for putting me in the middle of this shit, but now I just wanted the whole thing to be over. I had expected a quiet and relaxing weekend, but instead, I was and on my way to jail for punching out my boyfriend's man.

"Perfect!!! This is the absolute perfect way to cap off a totally jacked up weekend." I thought out loud as I walked with Officer Jones to the police car parked immediately outside of the window from which I had enjoyed the breeze earlier, while wondering if Gerald was for real.

I rode in the front seat of the police car on the way to the precinct as Officer Jones drove and his partner, Jack, sat behind us in the back. Jack initially protested but backed off as Office Jones or Darryl as he later told me he liked to be called, pulled rank and became insistent. I don't know if I was just bitter at Gerald, and thus white folk in general, or what, but it did my heart good to see a brother with that much control. And I was glad "Jack" had to sit

44

his ass in the back.

By the time we got to the station Darryl and I had talked up a blue streak about his wife, kids, his time on the force, having to deal with belligerent white folks in and out of the force. And I had told him about my job and how I sometimes had trouble with the white folks I worked with like Nurse Tamika who identified themselves as white, but had that one drop of Black blood in them from way back somewhere or other and therefore thought they could say anything they wanted and get away with it. Before I got out of the squad car Darryl had invited me to come visit his church which, he explained, was a traveling congregation and was scheduled to come to Jersey some time next month. He explained that they went from city to city setting up temples along their way. I was reluctant, but I decided that he didn't need to know that and told him that I'd be there if I could. He wrote his address and phone number down as his partner anxiously waited for me to get out of the car and for someone to let him out.

We stopped at two chest-high desks before I was finally led into what Darryl referred to as "the holding cell". Darryl explained that I would have to wait here until the judge had set bail and that at that point I would be free to leave, after I had paid the bondsman. I hadn't realized how grateful I'd been for his company throughout this ordeal until he said "O.K. well this is it. It's really not so bad, if you don't think about it. But, like I said I'll try to get your bail set within the hour and in the mean time if you have someone you want to call to have come pick you up, there's a phone on that desk on the other side of this door. Just let me know when you're ready to use it." I was ready right then and I asked if I could make the call right

45

then, because I knew that it was going to take Rachael at least three and a half hours to get here, as slow as she drives. That is if she was even home in the first place.

"Hello??" Rachael sang into the phone and as the sound of her familiar voice washed over me, emotions just came up out of nowhere.

"Rae Rae, it's me. I...I'm sort of in trouble...I'm at the Lackawanna County jail and I need you to come get me". My voice trembled and I began to cry as I was talking, but the tears were from frustration and anger more than anything. I briefly explained the situation to Rachael and waited for her response.

"Everything's gon' be alright, babe don't worry about anything. I'ma get Kennard and we'll be up in a couple of hours, alright."

"O.K. . . Thanks Rae Rae". I said, as I sniffled while trying to choke back the tears. As I got off the phone Darryl handed a tissue and tried to comfort me while escorting me back to the cell. It was a fairly small, cold, dank, urine stained space that didn't look at all like I'd imagined it would. There were no bars, cots, no toilet and I was it's only inhabitant. There were two metal benches which lined the sidewalls. The front door was a large metal one with a window in the middle of it that was about two feet wide. The rear door was made of some sort of heavy wood and based on the noise that I inadvertently heard from the other side appeared to be an entrance way to a courtroom.

I tried to focus on the drunk driving case that the judge was trying at the time, but all I could think about was 'what if Nanna knew where I was'. I thought to myself 'the shock of it would probably kill her.' For the first time in a long time I felt scared and uncertain as to what to do about it. I cursed myself that I couldn't stop the fucking tears as I sat on one of the benches with my knees drawn up to my chest. I wanted to go home.

The ride home was quite and I was thankful that nobody tried to fill the silence with empty chatter. I had wanted to thank Officer Darryl, but Rae Rae and Kenny had me out of the station so quick that I hadn't had time to think of him or much of anything else for that matter. It was about 11:30 Sunday night when we finally got back into town. We decided to drop Rae Rae off first because we all had to work in the morning and Kenny and I lived relatively close to each other.

I got out of the car and walked Rae Rae to her door so that I could thank her privately for coming to get me and to at least briefly answer some of the questions I knew she was dying to ask but hadn't.

"You're always there for me girl, no matter what" I said as I hugged Rachael tightly and felt a tear roll down my face.

"You damned right!! Somebody gotta be, cabbage-head. And if not me...who" she replied. We both laughed as I pulled back from her and kissed her cheek.

"Yeah, well thank you nonetheless. And thank-you for not asking me about it on the way home. I know you got some questions, I just wasn't in the mood to be talking at all."

"Gurrrl, I thought I was going to bust. Now you know a sister can't hold her tongue but for so long. But, really, are you o.k.?"

"Yeah, I'm fine. I'll tell you all about it tomorrow."

"Ok. You my sister and I love you girl. Call me if you need anything. Ok?"

"Ok. I love you too babe." I hugged Rachel and held onto her for a while, assured that if anybody ever had my back, it was her. I hurried a little to get back to the car, because I

didn't want Kennard waiting any longer than he had to.
"I'se guess, I be drivin' you home na' miss lazy" Kenny
teased as I got back in the car.
"Now, Holt don't you be sassin' me none, y' hear" I
responded in kind. I hadn't realized how much I had
missed Kenny's warm smile and seductive laugh until that
moment. It felt good that we were sharing the friendship
that we had once enjoyed on a much more frequent basis.
"Now, that's what I like to see" Kenny replied in reference
to my smile. "That, and two women all hugged up like
y'all just were….just hot and juicy sweaty womens all…"
"What's wrong, you jealous baby" it was my turn to tease.
"Seriously, Kenny I really appreciate you're coming up
there to get me. I don't know what I would have done
without you."
"C'mon now, you know, there's nothing I wouldn't do for
you."
"I know, I know, but it's nice see the theory in practice.
And you do know the feeling is mutual, don't you?"
"Oh, no doubt." There was a long pause and since we both
were beginning to feel a little uncomfortable about the
direction of the conversation, I changed the subject.
"So tell me about the new lady in your life, I hear she's
something."
"That she is!... Her name is Taylor Jordan, she's 28, she's a
nursing student, she's..." I was happy to have changed the
subject, and had zoned out shortly after Kenny started to
answer. I was thinking of what I was going to say to Nanna
about this weekend, when I heard Kenny say "...and Shay, I
can say without a doubt that she is the best thing that's ever
happened to me..."
　　　　I don't know why, but I felt hurt that Kenny had
said that *she* was the best thing that's ever happened to him.

It was completely unreasonable, but *I* wanted to be the best thing that ever happened to him. I mean, he was the best male friend that I had ever had and there was even some potential there for us at one point, although that was a long time ago. And as we pulled up to Nanna's house I entertained the idea of planting a kiss on him that would clear up his obvious confusion on the matter of *the best* thing. I decided against it, and opted for a friendly hug instead.

"Shay…that you baby?" I heard Nanna call as I closed the door behind me, trying hard not to wake her. "Yeah, it's me Nanna" I called back into the darkness. "I didn't mean to wake you up Nanna, I'll talk to you in the morning."

"Alright, baby. I got a plate for you in the stove, if you hungry. I'll see you in the morning sugar." I was happy Nanna wasn't in the mood for a prolonged conversation, cause I sure wasn't. I was even more happy that she had fixed dinner and kept a plate warm for me in the oven. As I ate, I went over the events of the weekend and tried to figure out if this was something I should have saw coming. I thought to myself that there had to be signs. There just had to be something about Gerald that should have tipped me off that I hadn't noticed before. *Well, no matter.* I thought to myself. *I'm through. I'm through with dealing with sorry assed men and there petty little excuses, their promises, their annoying little habits, and the stupid way they all seem to be able to rationalize their way out any situation. I'm sick and tired of dealing with the bullshit. The next man I get involved with is absolutely going to have to have more going for him than good looks and what's between his legs. Dick has gotten me in trouble one too many times. My new motto is that a man can't do*

49

anything for me that I can't do for myself. Speaking of that I wonder what I did with that box of stuff.

Maybe I am a little stressed

In the next few weeks after the incident with Gerald, I had thought about taking some time off from work, to put it out of my mind. Unfortunately, whenever I did have that thought, I had a severe reality check when I saw the stack of bills on my bureau. Besides that, I had made up my mind that I wasn't going to let the whole incident get to me. So, I figured the best thing to do that was to throw myself into work and school, so I wouldn't have much time to be ruminating about the bizarre little love triangle of which I had unwittingly become a part.

However, about six weeks later, I had to rethink my decision to plunge into work like nothing ever happened, when I found myself two seconds away from beating the ever-loving snot out of Nurse Tamika one day for one of her stupid, 'I wanna be down' type comments. She had been on vacation for six weeks and was back and in rare dingbat form. I was already irritated that she had so much vacation time to take anyway, but then to come back with foolishness was just a little much. Normally what she said probably wouldn't have bothered me as much as it did that day. But, I admit it, I was pre-menstrual and as much I wanted to deny the facts, Gerald had gotten farther under my skin than I wanted to acknowledge. Really though, the big part of my anger was just the shear stupidity of her comments and the fact that she felt comfortable enough to come at me with them.

I was just going over a patient's chart when she comes up to me, with this big grin on her face, and says, "Hey sweetie, how was your weekend with our friend Dr.

Gerald". I felt like saying, "well *sweetie* that's none of your fucking business, now is it", but I didn't. In fact, had she left it at that I would have just chalked it up to Tamika being her nosy-assed self and probably wouldn't have given it another thought. But she just kept going on. "So, tell me is he as good a lay as he looks, 'cause if he is, he can show me some of that bedside manner of his anytime, if you know what I mean". Now, I could feel myself getting a little hot under the collar, because as far as she knew, the triflin' hoe, was talking to me about wanting to fuck my man, even if she was joking and even if he wasn't my man any more.

Now, joking or not, where I come from, you just don't say stuff like that. Not unless you and your girl are just really really tight like that. Rae Rae could joke like that, because we're cool and Rennie could do that for a lot of reasons, not the least of which being that she is currently happily delving into her lesbian tendencies. But this chick just doesn't know me like that and she has to know that we just were not at all cool like that.

But still I was calm, and when I just kept looking at my chart, I thought she would catch the hint. Apparently she didn't. She just kept going. "...and oh, yeah, let me ask you something, Shay, cause it's kind of been on my mind for a while, and I just didn't really know who or even how to ask really, but since you my girl and all...it's been a long time since I've been with a white guy, and it's like some of the brother's I've been with lately, well, actually a lot of them...seem to have this, I don't know, this...odor to them. It's not really a bad odor or anything but, you know...well, it's been so long...I mean I just don't remember, but do you find that white guys have an odor to them?" Well, that I was just about all the stupid fucking idiotic chitchat I

52

could take and I let her know in no uncertain terms. "You know what, I don't know who you think you're talking to, but I'm not her! OK! First of all, I'm not your girl. And secondly, not that it's any of your business, but, no, none of the men I've ever been with, black, white or other have had *an odor*…perhaps you should focus on finding guys that actually bathe once in a while. And the next thing you need to do is to stop asking me stupid questions, because it's getting more and more difficult for me not to dig all up in your…suffice it to say that I don't plan on making this speech again, so please, think before you let some idiocy out your face again or the next time you're gon' think I was working for Exxon".

I heard myself, but I couldn't believe how much I was wolffin'. I hadn't intended to respond that way, but she had touched a nerve. And really she had had it coming for a long time. When I had finished, her face was bright red and she started apologizing up one wall and down another. And by the time she had finished explaining what she didn't mean, I knew that I needed to take some time off. Because the more she talked, the more she reminded me of Gerald and Kenny and every other trifflin' assed person in my life that 'didn't mean to...' And it just made me want to slap the shit out of her.

A couple of weeks later after I'd had a chance to calm down, I saw that maybe I was a little harsh with Tamika on that day, but I just have really not been in the mood for dumb stuff lately and to have to put up with her ignorant curiosity was just that much more than I could deal with.

Up until today, I've been doing a good job of avoiding Gerald or having to assist with any of his patients,

53

but I knew that it would only be a matter of time before my luck ran out. And, true to form, it happened right after lunch. I had been nauseous all morning, but I'd gambled that I might be able to keep a salad down and had lost, badly. In fact, I had just gotten out of the bathroom from what felt like puking my left lung out, when the nurse manager spotted me.

"Oh, Nurse Peterson could you assist Dr. Thompson he needs someone to prep for sutures; sixteen year old put his hand through a plate glass window".

"Sure. No problem." I said.

It had been a little over a month and a half since I had been around Gerald for any extended period of time and for some reason he looked really feminine and just downright girlish. All I could think was that I could have kicked myself for not knowing sooner and I guess he saw the look of my face and spoke up. "Oh...uh, Shay...hi...look, I didn't set this up and I'll understand if you want to get Kim to do this." I was in the process of telling him that that wouldn't be necessary, when, what had to be, the last of my lunch made it's way back up into my throat and I found myself racing to the restroom. I don't know, quite how Gerald took my having almost vomited on him, but I didn't really care, anyway. All I knew was that work was not where I needed to be at that point and so I took the rest of the afternoon. All I wanted to do was go home and get under the covers.

As I drove home I thought to myself that I couldn't remember the last special thing that I had done for me in some time. I had really been pushing myself with school, work and trying to take care of Nanna as best I could. As I thought, I came to the realization that I'd really been neglecting myself lately. I mean, I had felt nauseous for the past few days, but it took projectile vomiting for me to stop and just give myself some rest. I was tired all the time, I didn't really want to eat, I was irritable, and my cycle was even late and shorter than usual, which was rare cause I'm usually like clockwork. So, that settled it, I was going to take some time off and get back to me.

My thought initially was that I had hit it right on the head. I mean, it was only a few hours after I had decided to take a break from all of the stressful stuff in my life and I felt like a new woman. I wasn't nauseous anymore, I felt less irritable and I was even able to eat a little and keep it down. In fact, I felt so good, that I decided to stop by and check out Rae Rae for a minute.

I could smell the incense as I walked up to Rachel's apartment. I rang the bell and a minute later I thought I was going to choke on the billow of smoke that rushed out at me as she opened the door.

"Hey girl..." she smiled at me and held the door open so I could enter. Rachel's eyes were burgundy where they should have been white and the scent of the incense became unpleasant as I walked further into the apartment where it clashed with at least two other distinctive aromas.

"Damn, girl what'd you do, just take a match to a bag of popcorn or what?"

"Yeah, I know. You see I've got the windows up and I turned the fans around hoping they'd blow some of the smell out..."

"Well, you know the weed ain't helping none either, Rae Rae"

"Weed? Why madam I beg your pardon! I am offended at the accusation, that a fine upstanding member of the community, such as myself would engage in such nefarious and salacious conduct as imbibing and, how do they say, uh, 'totting up', this, this 'weed' as you put it."

"Was it good, Rae Rae?"

"The bomb!! Girl, you know I am tore up from the floor up."

"Um-hum, you lucky I'm not one of your kids' parents."

"Shoot, they know better than stopping by unannounced. And really, think about it, did your parents ever stop by any of your teacher's cribs, at all, ever?"

"Yeah, true that, but I never had a teacher as *therill'* as you either." That was Rachel's favorite made up word meaning thorough and together.

"Well, sho' ya right! You ain't ever lied about 'bout that right there." We both laughed and I told Rachel about the day I had had and about my decision to take some time off from work. Rachel listened intently and responded, "girl, you better not beat that little white girl up; triflin' as the heifer obviously is...but, how long have you been sick like that?"

"I don't know about a week or so, why?"

"Well, when was your last period?"

"Rachel, you need to stop smokin' weed. I am not pregnant."

"Are you sure, I mean, did you take a test or what?"

"No, but..."

"But what Shelita? But you can't be? Didn't you say that you and Dr. Reld got busy a couple of times before ol' boy broke up the party?"

"Yeah, but...but he wore a condom, I think..."

"Did you just say, 'but he wore a condom...*I think*'? And you want *me* to stop smoking weed! Well, baby tell me where to get some of that shit that you smoking, cause that

56

stuff has just gotta be some kind of wonderful." I hadn't
allowed myself to think very much about the weekend with
Gerald at all until this point and then it all made sense; the
irritability, the nausea, the vomiting, my having been late
this month, and it being a very short period. And then I had
a thought that confirmed my fears and as the memories of
that weekend came flooding back I confided in Rachel,
"...oh, shit Rae Rae, he didn't wear a condom, cause I was
on the pill and we had been tested together...shit! Oh, fuck
girl, I think I might be pregnant." I could feel the tears well
up as Rachel put her arm around my shoulder to comfort
me.
"It's gon' be alright babe. I mean, first we don't even know
if you are pregnant. Let's just get a test so we'll know what
we're dealing with, and then we'll figure out where to go
from there, alright?"
"Alright." I said through my tears.
"You gon' be alright babe...you know why?"
"Why?" I sniffled
"'Cause I ain't gon' let you not be O.K., big head...but first
let's get something to eat, a sister is hungrier than a mug".
I laughed in spite of myself and although I was scared, I
knew that everything was going to be O.K... Because, I
knew I wasn't alone. Even though I would have liked if it
had worked out that Gerald was there to help me through
this, it didn't matter, because Rachel was there. She was
always there. And she was more than a friend, she was like
a sister, and I thanked God for her a thousand times over at
that moment.

The room was kind of crowded for it to be so early
in the morning and the mood of the room was so sullen that
I was glad that I had Rachel there with me. There was soft

orchestral music playing in the background and Rachel held my hand the whole time which broke the tension and really did helped me to be able to relax, at least a little bit. I had never been in an abortion clinic and, frankly, I was scared. They had explained the procedure to me the week before in the mandatory counseling session I had attended, but that didn't matter. I just didn't know what I should be expecting and the only thing I could force myself to concentrate on was how cold it was and the scent of the Chamomile tea they had given me to help me relax.

Tea or not, by the time they called my name, my heart was in my throat. From the waiting area they escorted us to a small, even colder exam room where, after I exchanged my clothes for a drafty gown, we waited for about another half an hour. Through it all, Rachel was great. I hadn't said more than two words to anybody the whole time I was there, including her, yet she didn't try to fill the silence with chatter. She knew when to smile, to squeeze my hand or to joke and it all seemed exactly at the right time. Rachel had always been good in these situations and that was what I admired most about her; she knew what I needed, even when I didn't exactly know.

When the procedure was finally under way I tried to make myself think about *that*, and how fortunate I am to have someone like Rachel in my corner, but my mind kept drifting back to the tiny life I was about to... Well, let's just say I couldn't stay focused. So, eventually, I stopped trying and just stared blankly at the ceiling as the tears rolled softly over my cheeks and into my ears while abominable thoughts flooded my mind and threatened to never leave.

Prior to the procedure, I had thought that I would

feel a sense of relief after it was over, but now that it was, all I felt was an overwhelming feeling of dread, a sense of impending doom that I couldn't really explain and couldn't seem to shake. So, after a couple of days of moping around I did what I hadn't done regularly since I was a child; I prayed. I shouldn't say I hadn't prayed since I was a child, I just hadn't gotten down on my knees and had a heart to heart with God since then. I had said little mini-prayers regularly. You know, like 'God, please don't let this be the case' or 'God, please bless this food...' that kind of thing. But as far as actually just putting it all out there for Him, I hadn't. I think mostly because sometime after my virginity was stolen from me, I began wondering if anybody actually was listening.

Well apparently He was listening this day, because about an hour after I prayed, I got a call from Officer Jones, the Black policeman that had arrested me the weekend I went away with Gerald. He said that the traveling congregation that he belonged to was coming to my town this Sunday. I didn't hesitate to tell him I'd be there with bells on. I felt at peace when I hung up the phone. It was a kind of calmness that I hadn't experienced in a long time, my spirit felt at peace and it felt good.

Church of the Reverend, brother, deacon, doctor, pastor

I got a little lost on my way to the church and was about twenty minutes late when I got there. As I found a seat near the rear of the church, the sermon was already in progress.

"Let the *cherch'* say Amen..." was the first thing I heard as I sat down. The pastor looked to be in his late thirties or early forties. His outfit was impeccably coordinated, though it was a bit garish. He also wore a little more jewelry than I would expect a pastor to wear and his hair was conked and slicked back. His suit was kind of a flashy orange-ish color and his shoes were half suede, half leather rust colored Stacy Adams. Still, I told myself, no matter what his appearance was, the message was the most important thing. He continued speaking as I listened intently.

"...dearly beloved, we are gathered here today to get to this thing called life. You know, that's a 'lectric word, 'life' cause it means forever and I want to tell ya'll...that's a mighty long time...somebody say Amen..." Several of the members shouted "Amen" and he continued speaking. But try as I did, I couldn't help thinking *aren't those the lyrics to a Prince song.*

Nevertheless, I tried to listen as best I could, but it was all I could do to keep from laughing out loud at the thought that Pastor Pimp Daddy up there was only about five seconds away from just whipping off his jacket and doing that little shuffle step, that Prince did at the end of *Purple Rain*, all around the pulpit. But, I did get it together enough to hear the message which really was fairly simple and, truthfully, was one I really needed to hear. It was about not being discouraged in the practice of one's beliefs.

60

I looked at the program that I was given as I walked in the door and found out that *Pimp Daddy's* name was actually Dr. Terrance B. Sharpnack. And even with the rocky start, his sermon was actually on point for the most part and he summed it up best when he said "it's like this y'all, I've been up here talkin' fo' 'bout for'ty five, fitty minutes, trying to give y'all the good news, I say, I been tryin' to give y'all the 411 on my G-o-d and ya know, I needs me some water...What?! Awww, I don't think y'all heard me. I say, I neeeeeeds me some water! Somebody ought to say Amen, y'all!" The congregation almost all simultaneously said "Amen" like they knew exactly what he was talking about and where in the *Deer Park* he was going with this. He continued "...uh, but you know if I was the same way about quenching, my physical thirst as some of y'all is about quenching your spiritual thirst, I'd be soon dead of dehydration up in here. Amen? C'mon now! I think I just lost a couple of y'all! Ya see, cause some of y'all know that they is some bad...and I'ma even say some poisonous individuals out there just waiting on you! Huh?! They out there just trying to git you, cause they know that you is tryin' to quench yo' spirit's thirst, hah! And those of y'all that I'm talkin' 'bout...hah, and y'all know who y'all is...hah...I say, I don't want to step on nobody's feets...hah, but suffice it to say that...hah...y'all don't drinks nothinnnnnn! Hah!" The reverend dabbed at the sweat of his brow as he continued, braking the sing-song pattern that he was just in. "Naw...y'all don't drinks nothin', n-o-t-h-i-n, nothin'. 'scuse me, I meant, ...*i-n-g*. I know that's important to some of y'all. But back to what I'se sayin'...I say some of y'all don't drink nothin' and just pretend y'all ain't thirsty no how..." There were shouts of 'preach, preach on rev' and 'c'mon na', bring it on home

61

rev'. I knew the sermon was coming to the end because the organist was punctuating everything that Pastor Sharpnack said with a few chords. The good Reverend continued with his musical accompaniment and once again in his sing-song, "...But see y'all…hah…I knows the truth…hah, and your soul know the truth too…hah! I say ya soul knows…hah…that you *is* thirsty…hah…and just like…hah…I say, just like…hah…I can't say that because…hah…I know that they is some polluted water out there…hah…said I know I can't say…hah…that I ain't gon' drink me no water no more…hah…just like I can't do that…hah…y'all shouldn't say…hah…that because they is some charlatans…hah, some crooks…hah, some flim flam artist…hah…that are out there...hah… waiting to hoodwink ya…hah…to bamboozle ya'…hah? C'mon now…y'all don't seem to know what I'm talkin' 'bout. I say, just because they is some bad ones out there…hah…and maybe even some in here too…hah…that don't mean…hah…that you can or should…hah…say that I'm not gon' go be in fellowship…hah… I'm not gon' git' my praise on…hah…on the regular...hah…I mean it's wrong…hah…to just say that I'm not gon' take these shackles off my feet…hah…and quench my thirst...hah. Alright?! I say, is that alright??!! Hah!…I say, is it alright…hah?! Well, 'feel like somebody should say Amen, hah..." The Pastor continued on, but I was in my own little world. I mean, I don't know long he must have been waiting to slip the word "bamboozled" into a sermon, but even with all the broken and hacked up, split verbiage and *hah's*, I was kinda feeling what he was saying. I hadn't been to church in more Sundays than I wanted to admit, and there it was. He had hit it right on the head. Because the reason why I stopped going to church in the first place was because of all the hypocrites passing themselves off as men and women of God. I can't even count the number of times that ministers, supposedly happily married ministers at that, had come on to me after service. Some of them even did it right after having preached about the merits of fidelity. Or if they weren't trying to come on to me, they were standing so close that I could smell the alcohol seeping through their pores. And then there were the ones that beat their wives and berated their children so regularly you would have thought that it was part of their jobs, or that The Almighty Himself commanded them to do it. And then they would wax on lyrically about the importance of the family and about the children being our future.

For some reason, *Pimp Daddy* was making sense today. I had to admit, I had cut myself off spiritually for too long and I really was *thirsty*. I guess that's the reason that I wasn't at all put off when he asked that the *new comers* give a phone number or address to at least one member of the congregation so that they could keep in contact and help us to stay in fellowship.

It was Friday evening when Lester called and I had almost forgotten that I had given him my number. "Well, hello there sister Peterson" he sang loudly into the telephone and all I could think was *damn!!!!...listen Ned Flanders tone it down about a thousand, alright!* I mean seriously he was only about one 'diddly ho' from being a dead ringer for the *Simpsons* character's voice. In any event, he went on before I could respond, "this is Lester Gaddis from the Church of the New Covenant. How are you?"

For the next few weeks, I immersed myself in the church. Church was a part of almost everyday of my week. I neglected my friends and my family hardly ever heard from me. I was on a mission to know God better and nothing was going to get in my way. Dating was a bit of a challenge for me, because I learned that the elders quietly promoted polygamy. It wasn't right out in the open, but Lester often talked to me about his plans for his wives and family in the future. He would sometimes talk about the conversations the good reverend and he had had on the subject. I didn't really want to date him at first, but all in all, even though Lester was a bit of a nerd, he was kind of cute and he was the first man that had asked me out in a minute. I know it shouldn't have, but it made me feel sexy when he stammered through asking me to the movies. Truthfully…talking about the weather on one of the moons of Jupiter would have made me feel sexy at that point, but I digress. Back to Lester. We had been going out for a few months on Christian dates (i.e. no touching, no kissing, no nothing, NO NOTHING). Until one night we go into a discussion after the movie and I invited him to come in to finish our conversation. OK, I admit I wanted more than conversation. I had been celibate for about six months and I needed *some*! Badly! Talk about being thirsty!

   This night, Lester and I talked for a little while and then, as usual, he told me that he had better be going. So when he stood to give me a hug, I took my shot. I kissed him full on the lips and pulled him in for a very tight hug. I could tell he was excited, and best of all, *Flanders* was packing! I kissed him again and was quite deep in thought about all of the different ways I was going to be riding in a few minutes, when Lester interrupted my fantasy. "Listen…Shay…I really think I should be going, before we do something we'll both regret". As far as I was concerned, the only way there was going to be regret was if somebody didn't *do* me, tonight!

"Look, Lester, we've been seeing each other for a little while now and I like you a lot…" Ok, so I exaggerated a little bit "…and we're both grown and have needs and I would like to be with you tonight".

"Well, Shay I'm flattered, and I like you too, but I can't say that I would want to marry you right now, and I'm not going to engage in sex unless I'm sure it's right…so, if it's all the same to you I'm going to be going…I'll call you when I get home." Well, I must say that was a first. Here I am throwing myself at this man, panties drenched, nipples hard, ready to get some-kind-of-mid-evil-freaky on his ass and he says "…*I'm going to be going…*" . If I wasn't convinced that Lester was only trying to do God's will, I would have cursed him smooth the f̲ out. As it was, I was still annoyed. I had gotten myself all worked up, was majorly hot and bothered to the point that a cold shower just wasn't going to get it, and *Flanders* says 'I'm going to be going'. *Shit! I needs me something to drink, man!*

Things started to get a little strange in the church at this point, especially where Lester and I were concerned. He stopped calling at home and started arguing with virtually every comment I made during bible study. I had been struggling with the church wanting me (I should say, all of the members) to give away most of our *worldly possessions,* but the straw that broke it was when he said that my granddad was going to hell. Gramps was a Jehovah's witness and Lester's statement was "…well, then he's going to hell like everybody else who doesn't believe…". I'm not sure how I had started talking about

65

gramps anyway and, in fairness, I do realize that Jesus said that *no man cometh unto The Father, but through me.* However, my hostility toward Lester came from his arrogance and the judgmental position he'd been taking with me since he left my house that night. I mean, let's face it, I like sex. And even though he may be all virginal now, I'm sure he's gon' be getting his swerve on all the time with his many *wives* when the time comes. So, if the plan is that he's just gon' be doing a whole bunch of babes when he finally does settle down and release the freak, how is that somehow more moral or ethical than my needing to be broken off, by the same man-mind you, from time to time right now. Yeah, I know there's the whole not engaging in sex before marriage thing, but is a marriage to more than one person something that God condones. I don't personally know, though I doubt it. But, Lester seemed to think he was somehow better than everybody else; or at least me. It was like he thought he had the right to pass judgment on us mere mortals, (particularly *us ones* with, let's just say *more immediate needs*) when the bible also clearly states *judge not, less ye be judged.* I might have been able to get past Lester's funky little attitude, but when the church elders, *Pimp Daddy* in particular, began to co-sign any position he (or any man, for that matter) took, I knew this wasn't the church for me anymore. And I left. Lock, stock and barrel.

Where my girls at

Sweet! That's the only word I could use to describe how it felt to be hanging with my girls again. And even that word didn't nearly do it justice. Well, at least for most of the evening anyway. I have to admit that things got a little weird for me toward the end. But it's cool. Too much alcohol will do that I guess.

Well, anyway, at first it was just me Rae Rae and Rennie. Rennie's son Rashon was with his father the whole weekend and we were just kickin' it. Just the girls! Drinking, catching up. Well, mostly I was catching them up on my journey into and through organized religion and back. Then the oldies came on and we had a ball singing and just acting the fool until Rennie's friend Noel came by.

They had been seeing each other for a few weeks and I thought she was good peeps, but Rae Rae could not stand her. Mostly, she couldn't stand the idea that Noel was so open about her sexuality. I must say it intrigued me. Now, I've got to give it to her, Rae Rae tried to accept Rennie's bi-sexual-ness and did an ok job as long as the conversation never turned to that topic. And Rennie was good at not exposing Rae Rae to it, but Noel didn't really give a good damn about other folk's sensibilities, Rae Rae included. She was just a really affectionate person and she chose not to hide who she was from anyone. Unfortunately, Noel tended to hug Rennie a little too long for Rae Rae's comfort.

It seemed to me that Rae Rae and Noel's dislike for each other was pretty mutual. And truthfully Noel probably did do a little more than necessary, just to kind of piss Rachel off. Tonight though, Noel was in rare form. After she said her hello's to everyone, she put her arms around Rennie's neck, tilted her head slightly and started kissing like nobody else was in the room. Now, in fairness, I could see that Rennie resisted a little at first, but after that first few seconds, apparently she said 'to hell with Rachel's issues about this.'

The entire scene only lasted about 30 seconds, but DAMN! I mean, hands were groping soft and fleshy body parts and tongues were exploring each other. That 30 seconds was real! I had never seen Rennie kiss a woman, or anybody for that matter, like that before. And to be perfectly honest, I was a little warm from watching the whole thing. Rae Rae on the other hand, just looked dumbfounded. She had a look on her face that said, 'what the fuck do they think they're doing?!' She discretely touched my shoulder to indicate her disbelief and at the point that I looked over at her, her jaw couldn't have been more than two inches from the floor.

When everyone finally had their mouths closed and their hands to themselves, Rachel said flatly, "I gotta go". Of course, Noel spoke up and said, "oh, no, no, no, sweetie, please don't leave on my account. Please, don't let me interrupt y'alls' girls night, I just needed a little sugar…from now on y'all won't even know I'm here. I'm just gon' hang in the bedroom.". I had to pinch Rachel when she mumbled, "yeah, like I needed that mental image". But as always, when it came to Rennie's life style, Rae Rae put on her fake smile and said, "oh, no girl…it's not you…I'm just tired…I gotta get up early. You know how it is…" she lied. Rachel hugged me tightly on the way out and whispered that she'd call me in the morning. Rennie attempted an apology for her P.D.A. and gave Rae

Rae a brief hug as she closed the door.

"Damn! I can't believe how uptight that girl gets" Rennie thought out loud with a sigh as she put her head back against the door.

Meanwhile, Rennie and I continued drinking and talking about everything from religion to sexuality. Rennie was discussing her theory about the continuum of human sexuality when Noel came out to join us. And that's where the evening sort of took a turn for the weird.

Noel came out wearing a plum colored shorty nightgown and some Victoria's Secret Scent that I couldn't place. I say it got weird because the sight of another woman in a nightgown had never done anything at all for me before, but I could feel myself getting a little juicy as I watched her sit next to Rennie.

At first, I tried to tell myself that she really reminded me of a situation that I had been in with some guy, but the more I watched her, the more there was really no denying that it was her. She was a couple of inches taller than me, but a little shorter than Rennie and had smooth caramel colored skin and deep sexy curves. I'm thinking that it was the wine, or maybe the fact that I hadn't had sex in what felt like ions, but I found myself staring at her full lips as she spoke and wondering what it would be like to have her kiss me like she had kissed Rennie. I mean, I had kind of thought about it before, in jest, but in my liquored-up state, tonight I really did allow myself to wonder, if the softness of her breasts against mine really would be a turn off, or if I would enjoy their supple roundness. And without my permission, my mind started to wonder if I would be tempted to run my fingers through her hair or to squeeze her ass if she got too close, or if she has the same hot spots as me.

Again, I was a little more than buzzed at this point, and I couldn't figure out if I was I just drunk or if I really wanted to *do* this chick. I mean, would she be as yielding and frilly as she looked or would she try to dominate me and turn me into her little love puppy. I chuckled out loud, a little, at that thought.

At this point, I knew I was tripping. I was fantasying about my girl's woman. I snapped out of my trance when the conversation stopped.

"So, what...you don't agree? I heard you over there giggling...tell, me what you think" that was Noel.

"I'm sorry, my mind wandered a bit...what was the question?" I asked trying to focus again.

"Do you think that it's possible for a woman, a straight woman, to have fantasies about being with another woman or to even *be with* another woman and to not consider herself gay or bi?"

Oh shit! Had I said something out loud or what?

"umh..." I couldn't think straight. What the fuck?! Was she reading my thoughts? How'd she come up with that one?!

"Cause, no disrespect to either of you two beautiful sisters, and Ren baby even though we are only friends, you know you're the most wonderful thing that's happened to me in a long time, but Shay, I gotta say I've been watching you and I *know* you're attracted to me..."

"Hey, hey, wait...sweetie, I know we don't have a commitment to each other, but Shay is my home-girl and more importantly she's straight, so don't put her on the spot like that..." That was Rennie defending me, which would have been right on time, if the evening had not previously revolved around Johnnie Walker Red. Needless to say the alcohol and my horniness took over.

"No wait, Rennie. I can answer that, since she was woman enough to ask. First, yes. I do think that a straight woman can *think* about being with another woman, or even *fantasize* about it, but can she actually *be* with another woman and not be bi or gay? I don't think so. And to answer your last question, that wasn't really a question, yes. I am attracted to you, you're an attractive woman, but it's what I do with that attraction that determines my sexuality".

"Is that right? So, are you saying that if you have impulses to act a certain way, but you don't, that there's no underlying cause of that impulse, or rather that the underlying cause of that impulse is in no way tied to your sexuality?"

"Well, yeah…I mean no…I mean…" with all the blood having rushed from my head when she came into the room, she had me thoroughly confused at this point. And, to make matters worse, her intelligence was turning me on more and more, and all I could clearly think about was licking her lips.

"Alright, y'all this is getting too deep for me…I'm tired…I'm gon' get a shower and get ready for bed." That was Rennie and right on time.

"O.K. baby…and I'm gon' let it go…but tell me, how would you feel if your friend kissed me or if I kissed her?"

"I would feel like that would be her decision to make, if she wanted to…and I'd feel like it was time for you and your cute little shorty-nightgown-wearing ass to get off that couch and into my bed. And that you should be ready for some loving when I get there. That's how I'd feel." That's my girl Rennie, always there to help out, before I get in too deep.

"I beg your pardon! My ass is not little, thank you!" that

was Noel in a tone of mock indignation.

"umph…I know that's right. But little or not, I'm 'bout to wear it out…now, get in there." was Rennie's reply as she gave it a hefty squeeze and a hard smack, after kissing the lips I'd been fantasizing about since the first time they'd kissed earlier this evening.

"Anything you say, baby." Noel responded as she walked off toward the bedroom after having slowly looked me up and down one last time, winked and pursed her lips to blow a kiss.

In my defense, I have to say that trying to sleep with people moaning in the next room would be difficult under any circumstance, but add my extended period of celibacy and extreme sexual tension to the mix and I think anybody would have went and had a look see. I didn't think they saw me. The door was cracked and I was only there for a minute, but I guess I got a little caught up in the moment. Rennie was laying on her back with her head toward the door as Noel was going down on her. And according to Rennie's reaction, she was quite well versed in the art.

At first, I tried to tell myself that it was all academic curiosity, but when I found that I was touching myself and enjoying every minute of the scene in front of me, I had to admit there was something more to it than that and that I needed to go back to my room. I forced myself to stop what I was doing and go back to my room when I started to feel the first big wave coming. There would have been no way to stop myself from letting out a moan loud enough for both of them to hear.

About an hour later and a bunch of tossing and turning, Noel knocked gently on my door and then let herself in.

"Hey. I went to get some water and I heard you tossing and I just wanted to make sure that everything was alright. You left so quickly earlier."

"What do you mean, I left so quickly earlier."

"I saw you…standing there…touching yourself…you looked like you were having a good time. I know I was." At this point the pretty heifer was sitting on my bed and when she said that last thing she moved closer to me.

"Um…Noel, listen, it's just not that kind of party with me. And really even if it was, Rennie's my friend and I couldn't do that to her."

"Oh, I'm sorry ma, no disrespect. I mean, Rennie and I are just friends too and I think you're cool and I thought I caught a vibe…I'm sorry, I guess didn't. I'm not usually wrong about…I'm just gon' go now." The heifer had the nerve to touch my thigh when she was talking, not sexually, but a friendly kind of touch that lingered just a bit too long.

It had been about ten to fifteen minutes since Noel had left my room and the thing that had me shook was that my skin still tingled from where she had touched me. I had to smile to myself when I thought of her comment that she thought she had caught a vibe, cause for whatever reason and whether I wanted to admit or not, I was definitely vibing.

OOOOh, there goes my…

"Rae Rae, baby you're just going to have to accept
her for who she is, just like she does us…" that was me on
the phone trying to convince Rachel not to just totally write
Rennie off. It was Saturday night and she called still
ranting about the kiss between Noel and Rennie the week
before. I didn't dare tell her about my near lapse onto the
wild side. As high-strung as she was right then, she
probably would have had a heart attack!

I was getting kind of tired of hearing her go on
about "…that shit just ain't right, I mean how you gon' let
another chick put her tongue in your mouth, not to mention
in…". Thank God the doorbell rang at that point and I had
the perfect excuse to get off the phone. However, when I
opened the door, after I had gotten my heart out of my
throat, I wasn't sure if I'd been better off staying on the
phone.

"Noel!…What are you doing here?…How do you know
where I live?" Talk about a sister being shook.
"Look, Shay, I'm sorry to come by unannounced, but I
wanted to apologize for the other night. I was a little
buzzed and well…frankly that just does something to me. I
just think you're cool people and I enjoyed your
conversation before all the craziness and I'd just like for us
to be friends. So…I brought a peace offering."
"OH MY DAMN!!! I absolutely adore carob, how did you
know that?"
"Rennie."
"Look, I just put dinner on…there's more than enough…so,
you're welcome to…"

"Guurrl, I thought you would never ask, something smells delicious" suddenly I wasn't sure if inviting her in was the right thing to do, because I couldn't help but wonder if she meant the food or me. What was worse was that I don't know if I cared at that point.

"Umph!? Dang, girl dinner was delicious! You know your way around a kitchen don't you?"
"And a couple other rooms in the house too." I wished I could've taken that back. I wasn't trying to flirt with her on purpose, it just came out.
"oooo...k..., um, listen, I'm going to get going, there some things I need to do." *Yeah me too.*
"Oh, yeah ok. Look, call me some time and maybe we can hang out." Now I truly was trippin', but at that moment she just looked so sexy. I can't really explain it. I've never been physically attracted to another woman. I mean, sure I know when a sister is attractive, you know when she's really got herself together. But this was different. Last Friday night I could blame the wine, but I didn't have an excuse tonight. I was really attracted to Noel and I couldn't help but think that I wanted to find out for myself how soft those juicy lips of hers were. My head was spinning again, but the one thing I knew was that if I didn't do it then, it wasn't going to happen.

So as Noel was about to open the door to leave, I gave her a hug and held her just a little too long. I pulled back without letting her go and I could tell she was going to ask what was up by the way she cocked her head to one side. That actually worked out well, because it made it easier to kiss her. At first it was just a peck to test the waters, then I just let my inhibitions go and as I dived in, whatever questions Noel may have had at that point were the last thing on either of our minds. We held each other right there in the hall and kissed passionately. Our hands were exploring each other's bodies and as much as I tried to bring myself to stop and think about the fact that I was kissing another woman, or that she and my good friend were involved…it just felt too good to stop. Her body felt so soft and she was wearing my favorite scent. I always liked the smell of it against my own skin, but I never really got the full impact of it's effect on one's partner. It made me so wet, I wanted to kiss and lick her whole body. And that's exactly what I did!

I had imagined that breasts touching me would freak me out, but the way Noel moaned and arched her back when I kissed her inspired me and I licked and teased them while she touched and massaged her clitoris until she had her first orgasm. The other thing I thought would freak me out was tasting another woman's juices, and I would have hesitated in doing it, if Noel hadn't taken the fingers that she had touched herself with and traced the edge of my lips. I licked one of the fingers that had been inside her and to my surprise, I actually liked the taste. In fact her whole body tasted great and apparently she enjoyed the taste of mine as well because we didn't stop tasting each other until about 3 hours later. I've never had so many orgasms in one sitting. Noel said she around six big ones and a bunch of smaller ones. I stopped counting after eight huge ones.

Noel and I had made our way to the bedroom shortly after the first hour or so and as I lay there in my queen sized bed butt-ass naked and wrapped tightly around another butt-naked woman, reality began to set in. I had just happily and enthusiastically even, performed a lesbian sex act. All of a sudden, I hated the word lesbian. Rather, I should say I hated the word being used to describe me and my actions. I wasn't exactly feeling guilty or ashamed of what I'd done, just of how I'd have to describe it, if I chose to describe it to anyone. And in the middle of my thought, Noel kissed me again and all I could think was that it feels really, really good when she does that! I forced myself to stop thinking and to just enjoy as Noel got into position and took me on to number nine.

I did what?

I woke up from the best night's sleep I had had in
months, feeling around for the one who was responsible for
my restful night, only to find that she wasn't there. I
opened my eyes when I felt a piece of paper on the pillow
where Noel should have been. I inadvertently began to
smile at the thought of her as I read the note, which said,
*"Shay, last night was amazing! Believe me I didn't want to
go, but I have to prepare some stuff for work and I didn't
want to wake you. You looked so peaceful, so I just let
myself out. I hope you're not feeling 'weird' this morning
about what happened between us. I really want to see you
again, soon! I'll call you later. Noel*
I have to say that I was smiling from ear to ear and
feeling anything but 'weird' about last night, when I heard
a knock on the door. I cursed softly to myself when I
realized that Rachel and I were supposed to be going
shopping for a wedding gift for one of her friends today.
"Shelita will you please open this door, I mean dang! How
long you gon' keep a sister out here waiting?" That was
Rachel and suddenly I was soooo glad that Noel had
decided to leave early. I have no idea how I would begin
explain my new status regarding my sexual preference,
particularly since I don't really understand it myself.
"Girl, you need to do something with this doorbell…"
Rachel complained as I let her in and gave her a friendly
hug. "…um, hum, don't be trying to hug me and smooth it
over now, I've been out here for five minutes and…ooooh,
you got some last night didn't you?!"
"huh?"
"Don't *huh* me tramp, you got sleep in the corner of your

eyes which means you slept in and we both know that that's the only reason you ever sleep in on a Sunday morning…and, exhibit B, you smell like sex." Thus and to wit, that could only mean one thing missy…you got some last night!" I thought to myself *girl if you only knew,* as I ignored her query.

"I'm sorry Rae, my clock must not have gone off and I overslept something terrible. I'll be ready in a few minutes."

"Hooker, don't be ignoring me! I want to know who you got down with last night. I want his name, rank, serial number, and how big was the dick."

"First of all, I do not smell like *sex* thank-you, and second…"

"It wasn't that damned Gerald was it?"

"Oh, hell no! You think I would get with him again as confused as his ass is…girl please!" The words had already come out and part of me wanted to take them back as I did a quick flashback of last night. Because at this point I was living in that same pink and lavender glass house with Gerald and had no call to be throwing stones.

"Well, who then? You might as well tell me, you know I'm not gon' let you rest until you do." She wasn't lying about that. Rachel was like a pit-bull when she wanted some dirt. However, I was not ready to reveal my newfound preference to her just yet; partly because I didn't really know what to make of it myself, but mostly because I really didn't think that she could handle it. It was bad enough that she had to deal with it for Rennie's sake, and Rachel is not half as close to Rennie as she is to me. After the show she saw the other night with Rennie and Noel kissing, she might have a stroke if she heard about what went on in here last night. And to find out that it was with

79

Noel, whom she just flat out does not like anyway…oh, hell no! It just might kill the girl. So, I had to lie. I hadn't lied to my best friend in years, but it had to be done. "Alright, nosy…dang! If you must know it was Richard from across the street."

"…Richard Perry…M…Mr. Big Dick?…Richard from across the street?" I had dated Richard for about 3 months before I got involved with that idiot Brent. The *Mr. Big Dick* part came about when I started teasing him by calling him *Dick* when I heard a white client of his call him that in short for Richard. His response to me was '*I'll be that…but you need to put a handle and a 'big' in front of it'*. And believe me when I say, he lived up to every inch of his nickname. In any event, he was the only male name I had to give Rachel at the moment. I was prepared to come up with a bunch of supporting lies to round out the story, but surprisingly that was enough for her. I didn't expect that it was going to be that easy, but I guess Rae Rae just wasn't up for a sustained bout of twenty probing questions this morning.

"Hurry up and get dressed, please! Dag, you slow! I'm trying to be out!" I knew something was up with Rae Rae, but I couldn't figure exactly what. My suspicion was that it was because the tenth anniversary of the death of her mother and favorite aunt was only a few months away. She always gets kind of melancholy when it comes around. And that's cool with me, because she used to be downright self-destructive.

In fact, the first anniversary of their deaths, she drank, smoked, fucked and drugged herself until she was damned near comatose. Her mom and her aunt TiTi had died in a car accident that wasn't their fault on their way to pick her up from school for Christmas break. Obviously,

Rachael took it hard. That night, I had to stop her from overdosing on sleeping pills three different times. Until, I finally told her *look, you just gon' have to stop this, I mean, cause I might not be able to get to you quick enough next time. Rae Rae, you my girl. I've known you all my life and I love you like a sister. I don't know what I would do without you, Rachael. I know you're hurting, but I this is not what Lisa and Aunt TiTi would want. Look, I need you here! Your family needs you here! You can lean on me whenever you need to and we will get through this…and I guarantee you that you will be alright…because I'm not gon' let you not be alright.* It was difficult, but we got through it.

But like I said that first anniversary was a rough one. Rachael had been studying hard for finals which were the week after Thanksgiving that year and I guess the pressure just got to be too much because she went to a frat party, got drunk, used every drug that they had there and then let the entire starting line of the football team and half the track team take turns running a train. Luckily one of my male friends from the frat got wind of what was going on, broke it up and called me to come get her. At that point, I made her promise that she wouldn't use any drug ever again, except marijuana which she said helped to relax her. I still have concerns about her using that, but I don't bother her about it, because anything that helped her relax is a plus. And for Rachel's part, she swore an oath that she would call me if she ever felt like doing anything that crazy again. So far, so good and like I said it's been almost ten years.

I love Rae Rae so much that I really don't know what I'd do without her. She is truly my best friend and is closer to me than I imagine a sister would be. This is why I

81

knew I'd have to put some time and thought into breaking the news to her about Noel. It's not that I thought she would disown me or anything like that, but I don't want her stressed out, especially not around this time. Anyway, something was definitely up with her this morning. It just wasn't like Rae Rae to let something juicy go, especially not something juicy that I was into and that involved sex. Anyway, it was just as well for me, because I wasn't really ready for more questions. And I was more than happy to let it be.

Love should have brought your ass home

"…I have no idea what the hell you're talking about!"
"You know exactly what the fuck I'm talking about
Richard! Your ex-girl, my closest home-girl, Shelita
Petterson, the real place that you were last night! Is any of
this shit ringing a bell for you now?! You are not slick, so
don't try to play me Richard or should I say *Mr. Big Dick*.
Fixing your moms air conditioner, please…you are so full
of shit, your eyes are brown! To think that I started to
believe some of that bullshit you were talking about falling
for me, and…"
"Rachel, why would I lie to you about something that you
could confirm so easily! First of all, who told you I was
with Shay last night and why would you just blindly
believe that shit, instead of coming to me first?"
"She told me! That's who told me! And I believe her
because she's my girl, my sister…and unlike you, she
doesn't have a reason to lie to me! Men ain't shit!! And
another…"
"Hold up!! Wait a minute Rachel…look…I don't know
why your friend told you that she was with me last night,
but I had to go to Home Depot twice last night, once at
about 8:00 and once at around 10:30, while I was fixing my
mom's air, to get additional parts and the time is on both of
the receipts. I have the receipts right here and if you want
to call my moms and ask her where I was you can do that
too. Right here, right now!! You know I thought what we
had was kind of special, but for you to come up in here and
start accusing me and just go off on me like that without
even asking me, with no proof, no, no nothing…that's foul.
I don't really want to be around you right now, so you need

to go ahead and go! I'll call you when I feel like
talking...if I feel like talking!"

Well you probably guessed that that was Rae Rae
and *Mr. Big* himself arguing about the lie I told her earlier
in the day to get her off my back. Ok...now pay attention
because this is the beginning of a whole shit-load of trouble
that my having gotten with Noel spawned and it may get a
little tricky to follow. First, I should say that being with
Noel had been so easy and effortless that it felt like I was
dreaming, but after she had gone the dream almost
immediately turned into a nightmare. I was lying to my
cut-buddy...my girl...my ace...the one person in the world
that I knew would do anything for me and had my back
under any circumstance. Of course, I didn't know that she
and Richard had gotten together or I would have never lied
to her about having been with him that night. I'll get to
how I found out in a minute, but I was kind of hurt that she
hadn't told me sooner when I did find out. And really if the
wench would have come clean sooner...but, I digress.
Anyway, that was only a small portion of my problems, the
other parts were that the word 'lesbian' was not getting any
easier to digest when thinking about myself or my actions,
my conscious was kicking my butt about the lying and
about having been with Noel in the first place, and what
was worse was that Rennie apparently had stronger feelings
for Noel than she had let on originally. And so, of course,
that meant that I had to decide what to do with Noel and
whether or not I wanted to tell Rennie about what had
happened between she and I. Or at least the decision would
have been mine if Noel hadn't gotten to her first.

"So...Rennie...really, how would you feel if I got with

someone else?"

"Girl, why are you being so dramatic? Are you saying that you're not happy with our arrangement anymore?...What, I don't satisfy you anymore?"

"Are you kidding me...you did just hear me screaming at the top of my lungs a few minutes ago, didn't you? It's nothing like that. It's just that I know that you don't really want anything serious and that's cool with me for now, but I have to start thinking about my future. I mean, where am I going to be in five years, what if I start getting wrapped up in you and you decide you want to see another chick or a man for that matter...I mean, I'm comfortable with who I am, but what about a family. Rennie, I know you have Rashan and you've already been there, done that, but I'm only thirty-one and the older I get, the more I think that I really do want to have a baby...which means I only have a few more years left, if I'm going to do it...you know how I feel about you Rennie, but I need to start thinking about my future..."

"Look, Noel...I understand the consequences of my not committing to a relationship with you. I know you have to look out for *you* and I encourage that...you're a beautiful sister, you've got a lot to offer and somebody is going to snap you up...and you're going to make a great partner for somebody...hell, it would be me if I was in a better place emotionally. But *I* have to do what's best for Rashan and I. And I can only offer, what I can offer right now. So, if you feel like you need to get with someone else or you don't want to let an opportunity slip, do your thing. I'm here for you no matter what." According to Noel that was the conversation she had with Rennie the night after we had gotten together for the first time. Listening to her tell me about it was kind of weird though. I felt happy that she hadn't told Rennie who she was *thinking* of seeing, upset that she hadn't been more specific than indicating that she was just *thinking seeing someone else,* and kind of mad that she had slept with Rennie after *we* had been together. My emotions were just all over the place! And then there was the feeling of shame that kind of crept in every now and then when I thought about it too long.

So, in a nutshell, I wanted to have her claim me and to claim her and for no one else to know about us and to brazenly acknowledge our relationship publicly and to keep everything we did *on the hush* and to proudly shout about how she makes me feel when I'm with her and to hide the shame I feel about my *lesbian* activity, all at the same time. I know…but like I said, my emotions were all over the place.

Mondays

The phone rang at six-fucking-thirty in the fucking morning! And whoever it was, was catching the wrath!
"What!!!"
"Dang…my baby is cranky in the morning huh?" The voice was soft and familiar, but in my sleepy haze I couldn't put a name with it.
"Who is this, what do you want and why are you calling me so damn early in the morning?!!"
"oooh, feisty…you sound like you want to…spank somebody…" When I realized it was Noel on the other end of the phone, some of my irritation faded. Actually, the way she sucked in air right before she whispered *spank somebody* turned me on so much that I almost forgot why I was mad in the first place.
"Not just somebody…*you*, for calling me so early in the morning. I am definitely not a morning person and the fact that it's a Monday morning makes it that much worse. What are you even doing up right now?"
"Well, obviously thinking about you. But beyond that, I just finished working out and I'm about to jog my two miles like I do every morning."
"You work out…and then you jog two miles? Every morning? I hate you Noel."
"And I want you too."
"I said…"
"I know what you said, I was responding to what you meant"
"Oh, is that right?"
"Right that is!"
"Anyway…! How do you do all of this stuff before work?"

It dawned on me after I had asked Noel that question that I had no idea of what type of work she did. I knew she had a job, because I remembered her note saying something about having to prepare some things for work, when I woke up after our first encounter.

"…and since were on that subject, what exactly do you do?" I asked to rest my curiosity.

"Now that's a face-to-face conversation for when were both wide awake. I just called to say that I miss you and I've been thinking about you, and I was wondering if we could get together later on tonight…I'll make dinner this time"

"This, I wouldn't miss for the world, especially since you got me wondering about your profession."

"It's nothing to worry about. Now you try to get some rest, before you have to get up for work and I'll see you tonight."

"Rest! I'm wide awake now, thank-you very much. I will go take a cold shower though, thanks to you."

"Sorry, baby. I'll make it up to you, I promise."

"Umh-hum, you better! I'll see you tonight…O.K., around eight…chow, baby." *Chow!* Did I just say *Chow*? Oh, God I am so queer!

I hadn't realized how much I was beaming at work, until that damned Nurse Tamika got under my skin again. I had often visualized myself slapping the shit out of her, but today I really thought I was gon' have to do it. I mean, I had just been really cheery for most of the morning, which, I will admit, is unusual for me, especially for a Monday. At this point though, I was sitting behind the nurse's station, minding my own business, when who but Tamika starts with her comments.

"…well, damn girl! You just as happy today…speaking to people and smiling and shit. You must've got some last night." Now again, Tamika and I are not close and I thought I had cleared that up a few months ago. But just to resolve her confusion I spoke up.

"Tamika, that's really none of your business and way too damned personal a conversation for you to be trying to spark. We've talked about this before." I said all of this with a smile on my face, but unfortunately, Tamika wasn't the sharpest knife in the draw and seemed to think I was joking.

"…um-hum, you probably back to tapping that Dr. Gerald's ass again. I haven't seem much of him since he was transferred to Out-patient Ped's, but come to think of it I did pass him in the hall this morning and he was pretty damned bubbly. That's what it is, ain't it Shay, you tapping that ass again, ain't you?" Fucking unbelievable! She is quite possibly the dumbest chick in the world was my thought as my right hand unconsciously balled into a fist.

"Look, Tamika I'm gonna say this nicely one last time…stay out of my personal business! We're not friends like that and I really don't want to have any kind of conversation like that with you." I'm really not moved to violence that easily, despite what my history with Tamika and certain others might convey, but, this morning, she was taking me there kicking and screaming. "Well, what the fuck is wrong with you?..." *The woman just does not know when to shut up!* I was mostly calm as I stood in front of her and shifted my weight, ever so slightly, subtly preparing to punch her square in the jaw, when she made one of those ghetto-ass smacking sounds with her mouth, before she continued speaking…*that shit is plain annoying*

89

when a sister does it, but to have this scrawny-assed, little stringy haired, white girl doing it and moving her neck...oh, hell no! Yet, there she was with this foolishness. "...well...anyway, I just thought we was brown and..." And praise God that He still answers prayers, because my silent prayer at that moment had been that He not let her say another word, because I surely would have decked her. And sure enough Dr. Smith interrupted her at that very moment and asked if she would empty Mrs. Johnson's bedpan. Tamika stopped mid sentence and did not speak to me again the rest of the day.

All the way home I couldn't help inadvertently smiling at my thoughts about Noel. I thought about her tight body all sweaty after her morning workout and about being wrapped up tight in her arms again. However, just as it usually does, reality reared its ugly head again when I happened to see two unattractive partially bald goth-ish looking white women holding hands as they crossed the street in front of me. Before I knew it I had already thought to myself, *"Now that's sickening".* But the thing that worried me was that I wasn't sure if my thought was about how unattractive I perceived them to be or about the fact that they were holding hands at all. I mean, what about when Noel and I go out, as we inevitably will. Are people going to look at us and judge us like I had just done the two white women? *Shit! Why does life have to be so complicated? I mean, I finally find someone I'm genuinely interested in and it's a female. Things would be so much simpler if she just had a dick.*

My anxiety about my new relationship temporarily melted away when I got to my door and found three dozen red long stemmed roses waiting for me with a card that read *'because it's Monday and I adore your smile. See you at eight...Noel'*. Now this is dating! And, confused as I obviously am, the one thing that's certain is that this chick knows how to romance a babe.

After I found a vase for the flowers, I kicked off my shoes and checked my messages as I headed for the shower. The first one was from Noel saying that she'd be about 20 minutes late tonight, but that she could not wait to see me again. And the way I was feeling at that point, she was definitely gon' *see* me all night long. The next message was from Nanna trying to make me feel guilty about not having called her in so long (one week) after I moved to my new place. I kind of laughed as I heard the message *"lawd...my baby girl must've done met a man, cause goodness knows you ain't called me to check on me or nothing. I could've been dead by now, but you wouldn't have know'd it. I hope, at least, if you having relations, he relating to you right. Call me soon baby. Love ya, much...mmm, bye bye."* I stepped in the shower thinking of Noel and giggled to myself, *Nanna you have no idea*!

I opened the door and Noel and her hands and tongue made themselves quite at home. We managed to compose ourselves long enough for her to cook a slammin' dinner. Which was a feat in itself, because whenever I got a free moment, I felt compelled to come up behind her and kiss her neck, suck her earlobes, fondle her breasts...mmm, they are just so perfect. Anyway, dinner was foreplay that, while delicious, I was happy to see end. Because, after a whole day of anticipation, I needed Noel in the worse possible way...and she gave me just what I needed in the best. I was completely exhausted when I fell asleep in her

91

arms, still in disbelief that some babe could put it on me like she just had…no, correction, not *some babe, my babe*. As we laid there holding each other, I couldn't help but ask the question that had been on my mind since early this morning, "…so tell me my love, what is that you do." I playfully asked.

"You mean when I'm not doing this?" *She's so cute.*

"Well…"

"I mean, I'm not going to have to get used to the terms *bail* and *commissary* am I?" I said half jokingly.

"Everybody wants to be a comedian…are you sure that you want to discuss that now?"

"You said that that would have to be a face to face conversation, and, well, your face is here and my face is here, so…"

"Ok. First let me say that I do have plans to do other things in the future and I am working toward them…but for right now, I'm an exotic dancer."

"A stripper?"

"*Exotic dancer.*"

"Whatever, …you shake your ass for cash? OooooKay…" I wanted to let it go, but I couldn't. She was just too smart, beautiful and resourceful a woman to be doing some ghetto-minded crap like that.

"How long have you been stripping? And *(more importantly)* when are you planning to stop?"

"I've been *dancing* for about a year and a half and I do plan of getting out of it very soon." *Good!* was all I could think for a few moments, until the thoughts of men groping all over my baby began. She must has sensed what I was thinking when she spoke up.

"The customers aren't allowed to touch us and it's only a job…a temporary one." Of all the questions now running through my mind the one which most begged to be answered was

"…but how does someone so obviously educated and intelligent wind up stripping."

"Well, about a year and a half ago I was downsized by my job at Olan Mills…"

"The portrait studio?"

"That's the one."

"You're a photographer?"

"I was, until I was laid off. Anyway, I had a little in my savings, but after six months or so, I needed to find work. And I wanted something that paid pretty well, so I could open my own studio and maybe put a good down payment on a house. So my friend Stephanie told me about a club she works in and the rest is history. It's like I said, I'm not trying to do it for much longer. I've almost got enough saved to open the studio and to bid on the house I want. And I also want to take some courses Rutgers and maybe eventually enroll in film school.."

"So wait, among the other things, you're stripping to pay your way through school?" I teased.

"I know, I know…I'm such a cliché."

"But you do have a goal. I like the fact that you know what you want and you're going for it…but, baby, I don't know if I like the idea of men and other women too, I guess, touching you."

"Well it's mostly men, but even so, you don't have a think to worry about. When I am *with* someone, I'm *with* her and her alone…you were a bit of an anomaly. But anyway, what I do for a living right now, is just a job." I didn't like that line of reasoning, but I wasn't in the mood to argue, so I let myself be kissed and dropped the issue as Noel's love making dissipated my concerns.

93

I slept soundly and woke up to Noel quietly getting dressed. "ummm…good morning sweetie…where are you going?" I asked forgetting about my lover's routine of exercise and running. "Good morning, ShaSha. Got to go running, remember? Do you want to come?"
"Yes, I most certainly do, but that would entail you taking your clothes back off and getting back into bed." She flashed one of the sexiest smiles I have ever seen, before she obliged my request. And I say again, this chick does know how to romance a babe. Half an hour later, my baby was out the door and I was off to another heavy, orgasm induced slumber.

I couldn't have slept for more than an hour, but I couldn't go back to sleep, because I had dreamed about telling Rennie that Noel and I were seeing each other. And let's just say Rennie didn't react in the positive and sophisticated way she did when she found out about Thoroun. I made up my mind that I was going to have to tell her before she found out and I hated the idea that I was going to have to tell her about me and another of her ex-lovers. My plan was to avoid her, though, until I found just the right way to say what I had to say to her.

Time for some action

"Rashan! Come pick up this mess off the floor child!...and don't *yes mommy* me, either. I mean *now* Rashan not when you feel like it..." I never understood why parents pick up the phone yelling at their kids. Why not just let it ring or put the person on hold first. Anyway, it was time to talk to Rennie. Noel and I had been dating for about six weeks and aside from the occasional *I can't believe I'm a lesbian* moment, I was happier than a gay jaybird. Now don't get me wrong I wasn't ready to hold a parade and march down Broad Street, but it was time for my really close friends to know or at least one of them. Because, honestly, I still wasn't sure how I was going to tell Rachael.
"Rennie, if you don't leave that child alone..."
"Leave him alone?! *He* better quit working my damn nerves, I know that! 'Fore somethin' bad happen to him..."
"Dang, Rennie, it's like that?" If there's one thing I know, it's not to be voicing my, unsolicited, *non-child having,* opinion to a single mother. Besides Rennie was all talk. If she ever raised a hand to that child, I think they'd both fall over in shock.
"What's up girl?! I've called you a few times and left messages, I might add...where you been."
"I've been around, Rennie."
"Um-hum, I bet you have..."
"Seriously, Rennie I need to talk to you about something..."
"About the fact that you've been dating Noel for the past few weeks...?"
"Did she tell you? How did you know that?"

"She didn't have to tell me. I know you. You've been avoiding my calls, ignoring my messages, and obviously sweating about coming up with a way to tell me."

"I don't know what to say, Rennie…I'm shocked that you could know that…"

"There's nothing to say, babe. You're my girl and I know you. And no you didn't have to worry about coming to me. I love you, like my sister Shay. And I was serious when I said that I couldn't have a relationship with Noel. I will say this though…be sure that this is what you want Shay. Noel is one of the sweetest people I know, and she wears her heart on her sleeve…this is not just about sex or some type of experiment with her. I'm not saying that it is with you, I'm just saying that, she's never been with a man and she is looking for a mate not just somebody to play with…so, if you're not sure…" Sometimes, I have a difficult time understanding why I choose to be friends with Rennie, because she has an uncanny knack for irritating me. OK, what she was saying was true, but who died and made her the fucking moral majority.

"Alright, Rennie…well, thanks for the advice, but I'm going to get ready for bed now."

"Shay, you can be mad at me or whatever, but I know, you know, I'm right."

"…ok then, kiss 'Shan for me, I'll talk to you later." *Yes, she was right but…damn, did she have to be so condescending. I mean, why assume that I'm playing or just not serious? Am I not capable of true feelings just because I happen to be dating a woman?*

"Look Shay, I'm not saying that you're not capable of having real feelings for her… *Oh shit, did I say that out loud?*

"But what I am saying is that she knows what she's doing,

96

and knows what she wants from a relationship with you…do you?"

"Rennie I appreciate that you are trying to help, but why do you feel like you need to remind me about who or what I am, *all the time*. I mean, really give it a rest. Just try to be happy that for once in a long while, I'm happy."

"Look Shay, I don't care who you're dating. If you tell me you're happy, I'm happy for you. But think for a minute. Not everybody is going to be so happy when you tell them that you're in a lesbian relationship. How do you think your Nanna is going to react and, for that matter, how do you think Rachael is going to react. You saw her reaction when Noel and I kissed. Her uptight ass is not just going to throw up her hands and say *'hallelujah she's happy'*."

"So what are you suggesting Rennie, that I just disregard my feelings, because people might react badly?"

"No, I'm saying be a woman and understand the totality of your situation."

"Be a woman?!…OK Rennie your being offensive at this point. I *am* a woman and I have thought about the totality of my situation. I realize that not everybody will like the choice that I made, but I thought that at least *you* would understand it more than anyone else, even if you don't agree with it. But I see that…whatever Rennie. I'll speak to you later."

"Hold up! You know Shay, I'm sick of being the bad guy here. I mean, you do something stupid like sleep with someone else's husband, no fuck that, let's just say it, with *my* husband and I'm supposed to be the understanding one. Poor Shelita, got a fucked up deal, because she was in a relationship with a slug and now she gets to fuck somebody else's man, or perhaps even join a cult or maybe fuck somebody else's woman…"

"So now it comes out. You *are* mad that Noel and I are dating."

"No…well…you know what…yes! Damn right, I'm mad and I have every fucking right to be!! Why do have to keep trying to screw the people that are important to me? You make piss poor decisions about your love life and I'm just supposed to be here and understand. Well, I'm sorry, I don't! Help me to understand, why it is you pick everybody that's important to me to want to try have a romantic relationship with, when your shit falls apart. How did I get to be the fucking lucky one and I mean, who's next?!! In the next 15 years or so are you gon' be trying to fuck Rashan or what?"

"You know what, fuck *you* Rennie!" I can't remember ever being as mad as I was at Rennie at the point that I slammed down the receiver. *She is such a fucking bitch!* I started to call Rachael, but, like it or not, Rennie was right about one thing. Rachael was not going to take this well and I was not ready to open myself up to anyone else.

For about three weeks after my conversation with Rennie, I avoided almost everybody I knew, except, of course Noel. I didn't speak to my mom, dad, Tom or Nanna which was unheard of for me. Everyone left messages trying to make sure I was ok, until one day Nanna decided it was time to take matters into her own hands.

  Noel and I had planned a nice quiet evening alone and I thought it was her at the door until I screamed '*hold on a minute baby, I misplaced my key*' and got "*well you just take your time sugar foot, momma'll be alright out here*".

Oh shit! Nanna. I've had the worse fucking day, and I swear I'm not ready for this shit right now!

"Nanna…hi! What are you doing here?" I tried to sound as pleasantly surprised as I could.

"Well…baby they say if Muhammad don't come to the mountain, the mountain got to go to Muhammad". *Shit!*

"That's great Nanna!! I'm so glad you came by!"

"You not 'specting nobody special, is you?"

"Who…what…me…uh…no…no."

"Um-hum…well, child you ain't never been no good at lying, that's for sure. And if I'm the *baby* you was talking about when you answered the door, then you in some sad shape, sure-as-you-born."

"Oh that, um…yeah. Well, I do have a friend coming by to drop something off, but she ain't *nobody special* though." Oh thank God, Noel was not here to hear me say that. *Shit! I've got to try to call her to prepare her for this.*

"Nanna excuse me for a second, I was taping a movie in the bedroom and I want to check on it."

"Well, don't mind me chile', take your time." Of course my luck stayed true to its form and just as I had dialed the last number I heard the doorbell ring. One would have thought I was Gail Devers, by the way I hurdled over the furniture in my way.

"You didn't have to run back out here, I could've answered the door just fine."

"Oh no, it's no problem Nanna." I said through baited breath trying not to sound winded.

"Hey ba…"

"Hey Noel" I cut her off, trying to shout over her the initial part of her endearment that she always greats me with.

"I want to introduce you to my Nanna, Lilly Mae Peterson. Nanna this is my friend Noel. Anyway, Nanna just stopped by, unexpectedly, a few minutes ago." I said as my eyes pleaded with her to behave. However, her raised eyebrow

99

and the snide snicker that only I could hear told me that she was not exactly going to be behaving tonight.

"*Lilly Mae* what a pretty name. And now I see where Sha…lita gets her beauty."

"Oh, thank you child. You just a sweet as can be. Now I'm not interrupting y'alls plans or nothing am I."

"Oh no not at all miss Lilly Mae, I just stopped by to say hi to Shelita. I didn't really have any plans for tonight, except to curl up on the couch with a good movie." I shot her a look for that one. But I don't think Nanna noticed.

"You sound just like my grandbaby here. As pretty as you both are, y'all need to go on out and find a man so you can have someone to curl up with."

"Nanna, don't start!"

"I'm just saying…"

"I know what you were just saying Nanna." It's like no matter where she is or who she's with Nanna always manages to work up to comment about me getting married and starting a family.

"You know I ain't got much time left, I just wanna know when I'm gon' have me some great-grandbabies running around here. I don't think that's too much to ask, is it Noel?"

"Not at all Ms. Lilly Mae. I was wondering the same thing myself."

"You keep out of this. And as far as your not having much time, I don't know any such thing Nanna, you gon' be around forever." This was always my favorite way of shutting her up.

"I'm not talking about the after-life, I'm talking about right here right now."

"That's what I'm talking about too Nanna. You gon' live forever." She hated when I said stuff like that. I think she

100

thought it was akin to blasphemy on some level, but couldn't say why or how it was.

"Hush all that crazy talk girl! All right I'll let it go."

Nanna stayed for dinner and invited Noel to do the same. Noel apparently found this to be a good opportunity to grope and caress me whenever we were alone or when Nanna wasn't looking. I wasn't exactly comfortable with it, because I didn't want to think about Nanna walking in unexpectedly and catching another woman with her hands up under my clothing and fondling things that should be the domain of a man. I don't know why, but the thrill of being caught made me wet and I was so turned on by the time dinner was over that I slipped Noel the spare key and made her promise to be butt naked in bed when I got back from dropping Nanna off at home, not that I had to twist her arm or anything.

Noel's body twisted as her legs closed tightly around the sides of my head as I exacted my "revenge" on her for not being able to respond the way I wanted to when Nanna was in the apartment. She tried to push my head away as her legs trembled involuntarily, which meant that she was coming and at the moment her body was way too sensitive for me continue stimulating her clitoris, or to even touch her anywhere, as I had been doing. Normally, I would have backed off until she was able to handle being touched again, but not this time. It was my turn to be a little naughty and I just continued doing what I was doing. I enjoyed seeing her loose the ability to speak, which is also where I got my nickname a few weeks ago. I hadn't yet known that her body got that sensitive all over after orgasm and had simply continued what I had been doing. She was pushing my shoulders back as she tired to escape my tongue and simultaneously trying to say my name, but could only get out Sha…Sha, as she panted; which I took to mean she was just really enjoying herself. Who knew? "Oh, don't stop now, ShaSha!" That was Noel talking smack after the last wave of involuntary spasms had hit her and she regained the ability to speak.

"Oh, yeah like you could take some more."

"I can handle whatever else you got, baby!" Baby girl is always talking smack. I decided to call her bluff.

"Sike…sike…sike…ok…ok…you win this round! You the woman, Ma. Just hold me and don't ever let me go."

"My thoughts exactly." And at that moment I had no plans on letting her go, ever.

Here comes the bride

It's funny what they say about the best laid plans. Because being with Noel makes me happier than I have ever been in my life. Well, most times anyway. Yet, even so and as much as I hate to admit it, there are still those times when I feel ashamed. Ashamed of me, her, us...you name it, I've been ashamed of it. But when I'm able to put the thought of us being 'wrong' out of my mind, I am truly happy. The trouble is that, being able to put our wrong-ed-ness out of my mind, is getting progressively more difficult and now with Kenny's wedding coming up, I've got some decisions to make. I want to take Noel as my date and I know she wants to go. But I don't know how I can do that without loudly and clearly proclaiming something that I'm not ready to.

It's not that she's pressuring me in any way, but I know it must hurt her that I have yet to claim her in public. I mean, for her it's different, she's always liked women. There's never been an expectation of anything different. When she introduces me to her friends (I've met three so far), she does so as her girlfriend not just as a friend who happens to be female. On the other hand, that is exactly how I introduce her; as my 'friend'. There's no public display of affection, no touching, no holding hands and absolutely, positively no kissing of any kind in public at all, period, point blank, end of story. She says she understands, but for someone as affectionate as she, I know it must be tearing her up inside. I want to do right by her, but I can't bring myself to be outed just yet. Heck, I can't even stand applying the terms outed, gay, or lesbian to us or anything we're doing or have done. Normally this would be a good

*time to pick up the phone and talk to Rachael for some
advise, but I still haven't even gotten up the nerve to tell
her yet and we also haven't been as close lately as we once
were. It seems like we haven't even really talked much at
all since the morning after Noel and I first got together two
months ago.* The phone snapped me out of my thoughts.
"Heeeey, Baby" her voice makes me melt sometimes.
"Hey, sweetie. I was just thinking about you."
"Is that right? And what specifically were you thinking,
ShaSha"
"That I want you...to come...over me, I meant here...over
here. I want you to come over here tonight."
"Um-hum...so you're inviting me over for a booty call?"
"Yeah, you got a problem with that?"
"Nope, be by in about a half."
"See you then." The phone rang just as I had hung up with
Noel.
"Yes, baby" I said as I picked it up thinking that it was
Noel calling back.
"Well, I guess you were expecting someone else huh?"
"Hey Rae Rae! I was just thinking about you."
"Well feel free to pick up a phone when that happens."
"I know, I know...I haven't been a very good friend
lately."
"That's alright, I guess I haven't either...but listen, I need
to talk to you. Can I come by tonight?"
"Yeah, sure. Are you ok? What's wrong?"
"I'm fine, I'll tell you when I get there ok?"
"Alright. What time do you think you'll be here."
"Around 10. Is that alright?"
"Yeah, that's fine. I'll see you then. Are you sure you're
ok...you don't sound to well"
"Yeah, I'm fine. I'll tell you about the whole thing when I

get there."

"Ok. I'll see you when you get here." I was a little worried about Rachael. I hadn't heard her sound that down in a while and it was never good when she sounded the way she did. I tried to call Noel to cancel with her, but she didn't answer and her voicemail was full. I wasn't sure about how I was going to handle them both being here at the same time, but I reasoned to myself that I'd manage.

Rachael arrived first and was obviously upset. In my zeal to help my friend, I completely forgot that Noel was on her way too. Tears started to silently stream down Rachael's face after we sat down on the couch.

"Is this about Annie..." Annie was our nickname for the Anniversary of her mother and aunt's death, which was coming up in a few months.

"No, its not that...I don't even know where to start. Ok, I've dating Richard Perry for the past few months or so..."

"Richard Per...Mr. Big Dick?"

" Yeah. So when you told me that you had seen him that night, I confronted him..."

"Oh, shit. Rae Rae I'm so sorry girl. I didn't mean to lie to you, but..."

"I know. But that's not the half of it girl. He told me that it wasn't true and even had an excuse, that he had put in an air conditioner at his mother's house that night and showed me receipts from Home Depot where he had to run back for different things. I halfway believed him when I saw the receipt, but I still had some doubts about him being faithful...so one day I while he was at work I drove by his mom's crib. Well, it turns out she has central air, which she's had for the past 10 years. I had had my suspicions all along, so I finally decided to follow him after he told me he

105

had to stop by his mom's to make an adjustment on the air-conditioner he had put in. Shay, do you know I followed that nigger from his house back to my apartment complex! At first, I thought he was going to surprise *me* with the two-dozen long stem roses and balloons that he was carrying. But that motherfucker had the audacity to go to some other babes' apartment. In my complex! So this morning I went and introduced myself to her, as her neighbor from the other wing of our floor. She was really pleasant when I asked her about the balloons that were still floating around her apartment. She told me that her name is Trina and Saturday was her birthday. She said she had just spent a nice quiet evening with her man. *Her Man!* And then she told me that they have been dating for the past few months or so. So, out of curiosity I asked, who she got to install her air-conditioner, under the pretense that I wanted one installed too, and who should have done it but Mr. Big Dick himself.

"Trifflin' no good son-of-a-bi—"

"But that's still not all of it. I told her how we were both being played and we set it up for him to meet me at my placc tonight. Of course, he had to cancel plans with her and when he got to my place we were both there waiting on his ass. You should have seen his face when he saw both of us, but then th—" I had gotten so engrossed in the story that I completely forgot about Noel until the door bell rang. "That's a friend of mine. There's something I need to talk with you about too, but let me get the door, first." I still was not prepared to tell Rachael, but I had no choice, if for no other reason than I had to explain my lie about her *Dick* at this point."

"Mmmmm, I want you so bad…" Noel whispered in my ear after kissing me a little longer than I was comfortable

106

with with Rachael being in the other room. As I stepped back from her embrace she opened her dark gray trench coat to reveal that she wore nothing underneath it except a pair of orange three inch open toed heels.

"Oh my damn…I…um…my friend Rachael is um…umm, you certainly are naked aren't you." I was having a rather large degree of difficulty in thinking let alone speaking.

"uh-huh, what about her baby?" That was Noel as she moved in closer and began kissing me again. I snapped out of my trance when I heard Rachael clear her throat, obviously standing at the end of the corridor. *Shit!*

"Oh, hey, how you doing…why didn't you tell me you had company girl…" That was Noel again trying to close her coat and back away at the same time as though we had not just been five seconds from doing the booty on the floor.

"I was trying to…" I replied half under my breath though a forced smile.

"You remember my friend Rachael. Rachael this is N—"

"Noel, yeah I remember from Rennie's the other time. Um, listen, Shay can I speak to you for a minute in private." And with that went any hopes that she might not have seen us tongue dancing.

"Look, Rae Rae…"

" Shay, you know me. I don't beat around the bush when it's important, so can I ask why that skeezer is naked in your apartment with her tongue down your throat."

"First, she's not a skeezer and…"

"Well the jury's still out on that one…the orange heels say otherwise, but even so, why does any chick have her tongue in your mouth?"

"Yeah, well that's what I wanted to talk to you about. We've been dating for the past few months and…"

"Dating?! You and her?! That explains why you lied

107

about Richard. I don't believe…why would you not have just told me the truth?"

"Look Rae Rae, I'm sorry I lied about Richard, but I didn't know you were dating him. You kept that from me…"

"Yes, I kept who I was dating from you…not the fact that I get turned on by women…"

"Woman…not women. She is the only woman that I've been with and the only one I've ever wanted to be with."

"Um-hum, and I'm supposed to believe that *she* is just so sexy with *hers* that *she* made you have to have *her* when you've never even considered being with any other woman. Please!"

"Are you supposed to believe it?! Yes, you're supposed to believe it, because it's true and because I'm your best friend."

"Yeah, well…I guess that's who you are. I thought I knew who you were until five minutes ago when I saw you tongue kissing a naked woman in a trench coat."

"So now you're questioning our friendship?"

"Now, I'm questioning who you are. I don't know anymore."

"I'm the same person I was before five minutes ago, when I was offering you a shoulder to cry on…the same person I've always been…and Rachael, the biggest reason I didn't tell you, is that I couldn't stand to see *that* look on your face. The one that you had watching Rennie kiss her…the one that you had five minutes ago, the one you've got right now as a matter of fact."

"What kind of look am I supposed to have Shay? Am I supposed to be happy that my best friend is a lesbian?"

"You're supposed to be happy that I am who I am, and *that*, whatever it is, is *supposed* to be enough."

"Yeah, well…maybe it's not. I gotta go. I'll speak to you

later." Rachael quickly gathered her things and left quietly without saying another word. And I feel like I had been hit in the stomach as I collapsed and sobbed in Noel's arms until I feel asleep.

Kenny and Taylor's wedding was the most beautiful wedding that I've ever seen. It's not that it was anything spectacular esthetically, but the way the looked at each other just made me want to cry. I want that so much in my life. Well, in fairness, I think I may have that in Noel, but I can't show it off in public. I can't tell people about it, I can't even tell the people that are closest to me, at least not the ones that don't already know, about it. So I guess that means I really don't have it. I hate being this confused! I just finished re-reading *The souls of black folks* by W.E.B. DuBois and although he meant something entirely different, his words seem so on point to my situation. My whole life up to this point can be summed up in his words, *one ever feels his two-ness...two souls, two thoughts, two un-reconciled strivings; two warring ideals in one dark body...* I mean, here I am at this beautiful ceremony with someone I love deeply, but I'm miserable. There are times that I want desperately to cling to her, but something inside just won't let me, not totally. To my credit, I was at least able to get up the nerve to take her as my guest. After the way she comforted me in the aftermath of the Rachael incident, I would have never been able to forgive myself for not taking her. She didn't push the issue and I know she's got my back...she's always got my back. But, be that as it may, I still introduced Noel as my *friend* (not my lover or partner) and made up a story about *my man* canceling out at the last minute, when she wasn't in earshot. I feel like a heel for doing it and I wish I could proclaim my love for my mate, like Kenny and Taylor, but I can't. And I might never be able to. The more we progress, the more I realize that there are some hard truths that I'm going have to get used to, not the least of which being the simple fact that, if I continue to be with Noel, there is never going to be a white dress or any of the excitement surrounding a wedding. And I'm just going to have to reconcile myself to that fact, if we're going to remain a couple. *If we're going to remain a couple.* In the four and a half months that Noel and I have been together, the thought has been creeping into my mind more and more, and I feel a little guilty that I'm having it, at this point. Noel is the best, most caring and most attentive person I know, not to mention the best lover I've ever had, in every way. In fact, if she were a man I *would* be planning my own wedding at this point, or at the very least considering it. Unfortunately, she isn't…

"So am I gon' get a dance at my own wedding or what?" Kenny's voice intruded on my thoughts.

"You know you are…I don't even know why you would ask something like that…" Just as Kenny and I made it out to the dance floor, the song changed to something very slow. Kenny glanced over to find his new bride who was about to dance with her father and waved us on. I looked around to see that Noel was coming off the floor and had playfully raised an eyebrow at me as though she were questioning my actions. I winked my reply and hoped that she wouldn't be tripping later.

A man had not held me in quite some time and much as I hate to admit it, I liked it. I liked it a lot. Even though Kenny and I were only friends and had long decided not to be anything more, I liked how strong his arms felt

110

holding me. I liked the subtle scent of his cologne and most of all I liked the feel of the big bulge in his pants that was poking at me. I started to make a smart comment about it, but decided it better to not ruin the moment. Instead, I closed my eyes and allowed myself to enjoy being taken to a place I hadn't been in too long a while.

Noel and I hadn't said much to each other on the way home. I was still wrapped up my thoughts and extremely aroused when we made our way to my bedroom to change out of our wedding attire. We undressed in silence until Noel spoke.

"That was some wedding huh?" Somehow I knew what was coming next.

"Yeah, it was really great! I've never seen Kenny so happy. They make a great couple!"

"Shelita…can I ask you a question?" Nothing good ever followed her calling me *Shelita.*

"*Shelita?* Umph…this must be serious. What's your question, baby?" I braced myself for the worst.

"Do you ever miss being with a man?" *Shit!* Suddenly I became keenly aware of the fact that I wasn't getting any tonight and maybe not for the next few nights depending on how I answered.

"Why do you ask that?" I tried to stall while I thought of a good answer.

"Because I watched you dancing with Kenny. Your eyes were closed and you looked so comfortable…so peaceful…like everything was alright with the world there in his arms." Well, damn, she did have a way with words.

"Umm—"

"Because, I never see you looking that peaceful when we're together. Well, after you've had an orgasm, you do. But

111

most of the other time, you seem like you're holding something back."

"Holding something back?..."

"Like you're afraid of fully committing to us."

"Well…Noel…truthfully this is still very new to me. I've never felt, about a woman, the way I feel about you. I've never felt it about anybody for that matter. So, I am scared. I'm scared of being hurt, scared of falling harder for you than you will for me, and truthfully…I'm scared of what people will say about me, about us."

"People like Rae Rae."

"Well, yeah, for one…but also people like Nanna, my parents, my brother, the rest of my family. And I'm scared that I might not be able to have the kind of family I want. What if I want to have children one day? I mean, how do I explain the way I feel about you to a tiny little inquisitive person, when I don't even fully understand it myself."

"I see…" That always meant that she was done with the conversation.

"Noel please don't shut down on me. Now is the time that we need to talk. I didn't mean to offend you and I do want to be with you. It wouldn't be this hard if I didn't. I love you…you Noel…of all the people in the world, I love *you*. And I just don't know how to deal with that."

"Baby what is there to deal with? You love me and I love you and that's all that should matter. Not what people are gonna say or do. All that should matter is our love. Period, point blank, end of story."

"Noel, honey, you know it's not that simple."

"Then tell me how it is Shelita."

"Would you stop calling me that!"

"Tell me how it is ShaSha."

"It's complicated, and baby I will sort it out. I just need

112

some time. Can you give me that?"

"Shay, I've been giving you time. I take it, when you introduce me as your friend, and when I can't touch you in public, and when you make up excuses about your *ignorant-assed man* who stood you up a the last minute when we go out together. But how long is enough? How long do you expect me to take it, Shay? There is nothing I won't do for you ShaSha, including condoning your being with a man from time to time, if you need that...but how long am I supposed to wait for you to publicly acknowledge the importance of my role in your life?"

"I don't know. I just know that you are the only one in the world that I want to be with right now and..."

"Right now?"

"That's not what I meant. I mean, I don't want anyone else. Just please bare with me a little longer, until I get my shit together. Can you do that for me?"

"I'll do the best I can ShaSha, but the minute you start lying to me or to yourself about how you feel, I'm out."

"Fair enough. I love you Noel. More than I've ever loved anyone...and..."

"And what?"

"...And I want some of that na-na, so give it up baby." Noel screamed as I chased her into the living room and finally caught up to her in front of the couch where we made love until we both fell asleep.

When I woke up a couple of hours later, Noel was gently stoking my hair and smiling as she had been watching me sleep.

"Hey..." my voice cracked as I tried to speak. I cleared my throat and asked, "how long have I been asleep."

"I've been watching you for about 10 minutes, but I think we both slept for close to 3 hours" Noel replied smiling.

"Why are you looking at me like that?"

"Because...I'm just so happy that you're in my life. I've been in love before, but this just feels different. It feels so right...I'm just having a hard time believing it's real."

"You want me to pinch you?" Noel and I played together for a few minutes, with me trying to pinch her until she continued.

"I'm serious...Shay. I will do anything that you need me to do to make you happy. And, not to harp on it, I'm just putting it out there again, in case you didn't hear me the first time, if you need to be with a man from time to time, I'm ok with that."

"You want me to be with a man?"

"Are you kidding?! No! Hell no!! But, it's like I said, I saw you dancing with Kenny, and if you ever have a need, in that way, that I can't fill, I don't want you to have to do without...I don't want to loose you to no BS, that's all."

"Look, I'll let you know if I have any unfulfilled needs...ok? But, for me, right now it's a dead issue."

"OK. I won't bring it up anymore." As I lay there holding Noel, I felt a peculiar mix of emotion. On the one hand, I felt comforted and secure of the fact that she was willing to do *whatever* to make me happy. I've never had a lover that was so understanding and so committed to my unconditional happiness. But on the other hand, the cynical side of me couldn't help but wonder *why* she was willing to do so much for my happiness when we'd only been dating for such a short period of time. Granted, it was the same short period of time during which I realized that I was in love with a woman...but *unconditional love* is an entirely different story.

114

As bad as it may sound, and even though I realize that I lead Noel to believe otherwise, there *are* still some *conditions* that need to be met for this to continue to be a viable relationship for me...at least for right now, until I've sorted this all out in my head. And one of the biggest conditions is that we continue to keep the relationship quiet until I'm ready to tell other people and I don't know when that may be or truthfully, even if, that time may ever come. The two people in the world that I've told so far, the ones that I've expected to be the most understanding, flipped out on me. I want to tell my parents and Nanna, but I can't stand the idea of them flipping on me too. I know very well that a feeling can't be wrong and that my attitude *is* what it is, but that's where I'm the most conflicted.

I feel like I'm betraying Noel on the one hand and I want to let myself get caught up in the emotionality of it all. But let's be real, I am living an alternative lifestyle. When I look at her I just want to comfort her, to reassure her that everything will be alright. But truthfully I can't.

And if I'm completely honest about it, the fact that Noel seems not to have *any* stipulations or conditions to her love, worries me. I can help but wonder if her attitude is truly all about my happiness or if she has some self-esteem issues that need to be addressed? The one thing that I'm positive about at this point, is that if I'm seriously going to give this relationship a chance, I can't be about wasting energy trying to figure out something that only time will reveal anyway.

Guess whose coming to dinner

"YEAH!! THAT'S IT!! SHOW IT TO ME!! TAKE IT ALL OFF BABY, AND BRING THAT JUICY MONEY-MAKER TO MOMMA!!" Aunt Tina was in rare form tonight. Newly separated, after 22 years of marriage to the only man that she had ever been with, she was more than a little wanton. She had talked me, my mom and aunt Ingrid into going to a booty club after mom's birthday dinner left us woefully unsatisfied. We had gone to what was billed to be the hottest new restaurant around, I won't mention any names, but suffice it to say that it did not live up to it's hype; which really pissed Tina off. See, after three kids and more than two decades of marriage, Tina was what the family called *big boned* (not fat, but just the other side of voluptuous) and she loved good food. So when dinner didn't pan out, she suggested the other love—ogling good looking men. All throughout her marriage, as far as any of us knew, she never touched, but she *looked* like she was considering buying eye candy from Godiva. Tonight was different though. Tonight, Tina was legally separated and her inhibitions were gone.

"…oooh yeah baby…work for it baby, work for it…put it on me!" Tonight a decadent atmosphere and too many cheap drinks were Tina's excuse to make up for years of stifled sexual energy. I was almost embarrassed as I watched her make her way to the stage and use the dollar in her mouth as an excuse to orally fondle the genitals of Derk Dickler the chiseled chocolate Adonis who was on his back gyrating in front of her. That scene would have been enough to embarrass the hell out of me, if it wasn't for the fact that Ingrid, who been turned upside down and was being held in position by a stripper called Tripod (and for damn good reason), as he engaged in cunnilingus through her underwear, was brazenly stroking the third of the appendages below his waist as she held on for dear life. I had to chuckle to myself to see aunt Ingrid in this position, when I thought of her conservative demeanor and her admonishment to Tina "stop grabbin' on that man's stuff" before the first of her five Apple Martinis shortly after we arrived at the club. Yet there she was upside down and loving it. I must admit the sight of all of the sculpted masculine flesh turned me on something lovely, but my thoughts always seemed to drift back to Noel.

Moms seemed to be having a great time, although it had been a pretty quiet evening for her in terms of fondling or having been groped by strippers, which was fine by me, because I just am not ready to see moms playing in some stripper's crotch. You can plainly see at this point, that I am nobody's prude, but at the same time, I am soo not ready for that. In any event, the drive home was lively with Tina and Ingrid recounting their escapades with Derk and Tripod and discussing their plans for the rest of the evening.
"I know you wish Tyrone could flip your big booty up in air like that!" Tina started teasing Ingrid.
"OK! Guurl…but that is alright, we just gon' work with what he got, cause I'm fittin' to wear him out when I get home. So, Shay, step on it if you don't mind, baby girl."
"Ain't you nothing…" Tina chimed in, but was interrupted by moms.
"Uh, Ing, can we not get into an accident cause you want to bang your husband." I wasn't sure that moms was buzzed until that very moment. She never used words like *bang* or

117

screw and always thought they were crass.

"…I know, right, and besides, you know that if Tyrone had been all up in some hoochie's titties all night long and then came home wanting to *give it to you* that you would have a problem with it". Tina kept teasing.

"First, of all, he better not be *all up in* nobody's titties but mine, but if he was, he had damned well, better bring it home to momma. And Tina don't front like you ain't going to make a 'B' line straight to Michael for some, separation or not."

"Hump! I ain't frontin' I'm calling his ass right now."

"You two are a hot mess. Quite literally." I teased.

"Child we talkin' 'bout grown folks things, back here…"

"Hump, I'm grown…and y'all ain't that much older than me."

"Alright, now. I don't want you to get embarrassed up in here…" Aunt Tina playfully admonished me.

"I don't know why she would be embarrassed now. She done seen you with you face all up in the man's balls."

"Ingrid!" Moms wasn't that buzzed after all.

"You got a lot of nerve over there *flip*. We saw you *zerbert-in'* the man-man up-side-down style."

"Who?"

"Who?! You!"

"I was just trying to find something to hold on to…"

"Wit' your mouth, Ing?" We all had to laugh at that one.

"Jacq, I don't know what you laughing at…trying to act all like Mother Theresa over there. We saw you when the baby-girl was in the bathroom…" Ingrid teased.

"Girl hush up…y'all ain't seen nothing...and even if you did, it's *my* birthday." *Yeah, please hush up. I don't want to hear about mom touching or licking on some stripper.*

"I'm just saying…"

"I know what you was just saying…you just concentrate on getting you freaky self to Tyrone."

"Oh, Jacqueline don't act like Tom ain't in for a treat tonight too."

"I know right…you tryin' to be all low key for Shay, but I know my big sis and you just a horny as the rest of us."

"Y'all leave my mom alone, cause I ain't trying to hear about what she is planning on doing with my dad." Hoping I wasn't about to hear anything more about my parents sex life.

"You do know they still be getting it in, don't you?" Tina wasn't going to let it go.

"Tina, leave her alone." That was mom.

"I'm just saying, she said she grown an' all…"

"That does not mean she wants to hear about her parent's sex life." Ingrid came to my rescue.

"All I'm saying is that she should be proud, 'cause from what I done heard, her daddy could call himself Tripod too if he wanted."

"TINA!!!" Ingrid, mom and I screamed in unison before breaking out into hysterical laughter.

"Alright, I'll change the subject then. So, Shay whose the new man in your…" We had come to a stop and were waiting for pedestrians to cross in front of us when two uninhibited lesbians walked across the street giggling and kissing as they held hands. I was happy for the reprieve as I contemplated the new person in my life and how I might respond to such a question.

"I just don't know how two women could want to get together when there are all these men out here." Tina's pearls of wisdom just kept coming, but I was kind of surprised when my mom joined in.

"Tom and I saw this program a few months ago about how

119

it's becoming more and more fashionable to see two women together. Tom thinks it's because women, especially black women, are really are starting to believe the myth that there are no good men out there. But I blame the media. I mean, the more these young girls are exposed to this stuff, the more they think it's ok to just go around kissing each other and carrying on. They see it as just another lifestyle choice they have to make. The way I see it, the bible says to leave your parents and cleave unto your husband, not some other woman. It just makes me sick." Well there it was, out there in the open and I felt like I had been kicked in the gut. I had been trying to find an appropriate way to describe my relationship, but at this point any ideas that I may have had about telling moms about my new beau, evaporated with the thought her being sickened by my actions.

"I wouldn't just blame it all on the media. I think it's about society in general getting away from anything that even remotely has to do with the bible." Aunt Tina added. *This from a woman who not 30 minutes ago, had a dollar in her mouth and her face buried in some strange, damn near naked, man's lap.*

"I say to each his own, or her own in their case…" Aunt Ing…my girl…I silently rejoiced as I thought that finally, somebody had my back.

"If they want to do that nasty shit, let 'em. As long as they don't involve me or my family." I stood corrected. What started out to be a happy go lucky birthday celebration for my mom, ended with me having a sinking feeling in the pit of my stomach and my being thankful that I had not given in to my near lapse in judgment in telling about the *carryings on* of my recent *lifestyle choice.* Thankfully the conversation never returned to my new *man* and I

120

languished in silence as I dropped my kinfolk off at their respective hetero-sexual booty call locations.

Thanksgiving was two weeks away and of course Noel's and my conversation had turned to the holidays and family and spending time together with them. Until now, the holidays were always my favorite time of year. However, after arguing with her for the past three weeks about how to spend the first of the three major holidays of the year, I was spent and in anything but a festive holiday mood. Until this point in the relationship, the thing that I most admired about Noel was her capacity for understanding. I never felt rushed or pressured to declare my love for her to others, which I did freely in her circles. I can't front though, I think I did that mostly to let them other heifers know to step off from her…and especially that Stephanie chick.

Stephanie Johnson was Noel's oldest friend and had introduced her to stripping when she was between jobs. At this point, I'm happy to say that Noel had given up stripping and was working toward her degree in film. But, in any event, she and Stephanie had known each other close to twenty years and are really close. A little too close, if you ask me. Now I may be new to this lesbian thing, but I know pushin'-up when I see it. I don't care who you are game recognizes game. And I don't care what she or Noel say, I know that little Steph is trying to push-up on my girl. I mean, from the way she always talking about her and Noel's exploits in the old days. It's always, 'remember when we did that lap dance together' or 'remember that nerdy guy that used to spend all his money on you in the club' or just some other thing that I wasn't a part of and frankly don't want to be hearing. And if it's not any of that then she's always talking about how she's been there for

Noel, or she's got a story to tell about one of her or Noel's relationships that didn't work…or how Noel is like a sister to her…or how she was the one Noel could always turn to…or how they were both always there for each other *offering a shoulder to cry on. Um-hum, I bet that ain't all she would offer if given the chance. Heifer!* Now, I'm not gon' hate…Stephanie is cute…about a size 8, got some curves, and, as Noel would say, is her *size (*meaning that she has the body type that Noel likes in general). Even so, and not to be conceded, but she can't compete with yours true. At least not to hear Noel tell it anyway. I've got to admit I have wondered why they never dated, but there are some things a sister just ain't ready to know about yet. Besides, I trust my girl.

Still, I never knew there were so many beautiful black lesbians in Philadelphia. It's like now that I'm one of them, they're all around. Seriously, I mean, everywhere I go now, I feel like that kid in *The Sixth Sense – I see lesbians.* So when we are around Noel's friends I tend to hold on just a little tighter and kiss her just a little longer. It's like I said, I don't think that Noel is the type to have an affair, but a sister just can't be too careful. Because even though I don't think she'd act on it, I know she's still attracted to other women. On the other hand, for me, one of the strangest things about my newfound sexuality is that Noel is still the only woman that I have ever been attracted to. I mean, sure I will notice a sexy smile or a shapely figure, but I can't imagine ever enjoying being touched by *any* woman except Noel. And not even just in the '*I got somebody and I don't want anyone else* sense' of it, because quietly I am *still* very attracted to men. It's just that when it comes to other women, I'm just flat out, not interested at all. So whatever this is that I'm going

122

through, I know that it's about Noel specifically. She's everything I've ever wanted in a man…well, *almost* everything, without the non-sense. She understands me most of the time and, she's generally the epitome of understanding; especially when it comes to my confusion about *us*.

The bad thing is that I've found out that the shelf-life for *understanding* in a lesbian relationship approximately around nine months. Because as far as the holidays are concerned, Noel has, to put it mildly, been bugging! She has been, all but, demanding that she be allowed come to dinner at my parent's home, as my girlfriend! Now, perhaps I could have picked a more appropriate time and manner to inquire as to extent of her recent injury where she undoubtedly fell and bumped her head, but she had to be kidding. She knows better than anyone that, there are days that I don't even like admitting to myself that I am in a lesbian relationship, and now she wants me to broadcast this to my entire family…to my momma…my aunts…my daddy…my Nanna, whose already got a heart condition! Oh, heeelllll no! I can't…I'm just not ready!!! And I'm not going to! Now, granted, I should have been more tactful when I communicated my objection to that happening, but it just came out. So, of course, now she is seething. I hate when she is mad at me, but in this instance, she's just going to have to be mad, cause there is no way that I'm telling my family about this. At least not right now. No, emphatically NOT…I'm just flat out not doing it!

Well…Thanksgiving did not go well. Noel was not invited to dinner at my parents and we argued and then didn't speak much for close to two weeks after. She finally did start talking to me again and now Christmas is in five days. I don't know what possessed me to agree to it, but somehow, she managed to get me to agree to "coming out" at Christmas dinner. Actually, that's not true I do know what possessed me. About a week ago, she made a delicious candle lit dinner, wore my favorite perfume and put on the sexiest dress I've ever see her in. These are all things that I had done before to get my way in relationships that I had had in the past with men, so I knew what was going on. I should have put a stop to it in the beginning when I had a chance, but I'd never been on the receiving end of this type of seduction. Frankly, I was enjoying the attention and I was curious as to where all of it would lead in her version of the game. I wondered if that's how the men I'd been with got caught up, if they, knew they were being seduced, but only played along to find out where it would lead.

In any event, I found out *where* after dinner as Noel slowly undressed in front of me and then undressed me and kissed, fondled and caressed every inch of me until I couldn't take it anymore and had to have her right then. Just as I thought that we were about to get busy, she nibbled and licked my left earlobe and then she whispered *"don't think you'll be getting anymore of this until I get what I want"* and promptly got dressed and proceeded to cut me off physically and emotionally, until I finally broke down an agreed to her terms (i.e. dinner at my moms as my girlfriend). I couldn't believe how adept she was at sexual warfare, but I agreed unconditionally to her terms. In fairness, I did so mostly because she was right, it *wasn't* fair for me to continue keeping our relationship on the low with my family and friends. But I gotta be real…the other part, and maybe even the biggest part, of my rationale was purely selfish. I-was-hoooorny! I could barely move without my body reminding me that it had not been touched, by anyone other than me, in way too long. And the other part was that I really missed being with Noel in the same kind of comfortable way that we had become used to. Of course, we had talked during the time that she was mad at me and we had even spent time together, but it just wasn't the same. There was always an uneasy tension between us. But that was over with. Or at least it was going to be, tonight, if I had anything to say about it. I had the whole evening planned and nothing was going to spoil it.

The first part of my evening involved us going out to a club together. We had not been out dancing in so long that I thought I might have forgotten how. But as I watched the corny brother I was dancing with cheesing it up, I knew I still had it. We decided on going to a straight club, because I still wasn't the most comfortable in the *Lady's Rooms* yet. *Lady's Rooms* was a term Noel had come up to reference lesbian clubs while in mixed company. I just thought the term was so clever. I was in the middle of thinking *my baby is so smart and I am going to wear her out tonight* when my dance partner snapped me out of my trance.
"Is it that serious?"
"I'm sorry?"
"I say, is it that serious…you looked like you were deep in thought."
"Oh, that…no, I was just thinking about a friend of mine."
"Must be a lucky man."
"Who?"
"Your friend."
"Now who said it was a man that I was thinking about?"

125

The words had come out of my mouth, but I was having a hard time believing that I was flirting with the idea of telling a complete stranger about my relationship. It seemed like it might be a good idea, just to test the waters and see if I could do it. I convinced myself that it was going to be like a practice run. For better or worse, I was going to have to do the real thing in a few days.

"Oh...I...I just assumed...you're right, you didn't say one way or another." What had started out as a good idea, quickly faded when, for the first time, I focused and got a good look at the high-yellow baritone chatter-box in front of me and had him flash me one of the sexiest man smiles, I had seen in some time. *Maybe he wasn't all that corny after all.*

"By the way, my name is Maurice...Maurice Green, and you are..." *In trouble* was my thought as I responded.

"Shelita...Shelita Peterson."

"It's good to meet you Shelita." I tried not to smile too much, as I casually scanned the room for Noel. I don't know what it is, but she's got some kind of extra sense about these things and she's never wrong. I spotted her across the room dancing with some young looking hip-hopper, but I didn't think she saw me.

"Likewise, Maurice."

"Listen, Shelita..."

"Shay...my friends call me Shay."

"OK, Shay...would you mind joining me for a drink at the bar...I'd love to get to know you a little better." Everything in my head, told me that I should not go, that this man was just too way sexy to not be trouble in the making. Nevertheless, my defiant, attention starved body took his hand and said nothing as he led us to the bar. I felt a tinge of guilt when three songs later my rebellious body had

126

slipped him my cell phone number, which only got worse when Noel joined us at the bar.

"Heeey, baby!" That was me as Noel came and sat down in the stool next to me. I've never been good at hiding guilt.

"Hey ShaSha. Who's your friend?"

"Oh, yeah…this is Moe…Moe this is my *girlfriend* Noel." I leaned my head back onto Noel when I said girlfriend. I didn't mean to exaggerate the gesture, but I think I was kind of tipsy and I know I was very horny at the moment, not to mention guilty as a child with her hand in the cookie jar.

"Hi Moe. Is that short for Maurice?"

"As a matter of fact it is. So tell me what men in their right mind would let the two of you get out to a club, looking as good as you both do, without them?" I know Moe was trying to be charming and didn't mean anything by the comment, but I was equally sure that Noel was about to verbally let him have it full in the face, until someone asked her to dance.

"Your girl seems to be in a bad mood."

"No she's just got a lot on her mind."

"Is that right? Let me ask you this…when you said she was your girlfriend…you didn't just mean like a sisterhood, sister-girl, sisters in the spirit…kind of thing did you? You really meant *girlfriend*, like *I* would have a girlfriend…didn't you?" I was starting to get a little uncomfortable with the direction of the conversation.

"What makes you say that?"

"The way you two looked at each other and you were playing the pronoun game with me earlier."

"The pronoun game?"

"Yeah, it's where I say he or him and you replace it with

they or them...*and* she called you, ShaSha, which sounds
like a pet name, and you said your friends call you Shay...I
mean there's nothing wrong with it if you're bi-sexual...I
was just curious." *Bi-sexual.* It's hard to believe that in all
the time that Noel and I had been together, I had never even
seriously considered *bi-sexual* as a possibility in describing
my orientation. I was intrigued.
"So what if I am?"
"Then you just are."
"That doesn't make you uncomfortable?"
"Heeelll naw...why would it?"
"I guess some men would feel threatened...think it was
immoral..."
"Threatened or insecure? I look at it like this, if you know
what you're working with and you're good with that...what
else is there but comfort. And as far as morality goes, I
don't think it's anyone's place to past judgment on one's
sexual *preference*." Suddenly, I didn't feel quite as guilty
about giving Maurice my number, because now it wasn't
just about his sexy-ass smile, there was some substance
there. I didn't know how much...but at the very least, he
got me thinking...in the worse case scenario, we could end
up friends...and heck we can all use another friend. And of
course, I meant to say in the *best-case* scenario, not the
worse.

Unfortunately, Noel just could not see the wisdom of my
logic and let me know in no uncertain terms when we got
home.

"Friends? Please! Shay, at least be honest with yourself!"
"I am being honest! I would like for him and I to be friends
and I don't appreciate the implication that I'm being

dishonest with you."

"Yeah, and you know what I don't like? I don't like looking across the dance floor and seeing *my girl* in the arms of some man all night long, looking like she just died and went to heaven and then seeing her give out her phone number cause she wants to be his friend." *Damn! She don't miss a thing.*

"First of all, I was not in his arms all night! And second, even if I was, I came home with *you* not him…"

"Well, bully for me!"

"Oh, so that doesn't mean shit right!"

"No, Shelita it's *not* that it doesn't mean shit. It's that I have to fight for every little bit of public affection that I get from you and frankly I'm tired of seeing you giving it up so easily to every man that asks you to dance. And now all of a sudden you need to have some more male *friends*! If you need to fuck one, fuck one and get it over with! But don't bullshit me about wanting to be *friends*. Sometimes I don't even know why you're with me if you're so happy with a man's touch." That hurt, and at that point I wanted to hurt her too.

"Sometimes, I don't either." Judging by the tears rolling down her cheek I had accomplished my mission.

"I'm going home and you don't have to worry about Christmas dinner anymore…I'm not coming. Maybe, I'll call you later." And with that she was out of the door. I wanted to run after Noel, but my pride would not let me do it. She had hurt me just as much as I her, and truthfully on some level I was relieved that I wouldn't have to explain her at Christmas dinner. Still my softer side got the best of me and I called her when I knew she had had enough time to make it home.

"Hello?" Her voice sounded tired and weak from crying.

129

"It's me Noel. I just wanted to make sure you made it home alright…and to say I'm sorry. I was angry and I didn't mean it when I said that I didn't know why I was with you sometimes."

"Yes, you did. Shelita we don't say things that we don't mean just because we're angry. The quality of being angry just relaxes our defense mechanisms, so that we may say things bluntly whereas, we might otherwise sugar coat them. But we don't say things that we don't mean."

"How are you going to tell me what *I* do when *I'm angry*."

"Because it's human nature, that's how."

"It is not human nature, people are different and they express themselves…look, I didn't call to argue. I just wanted to make sure you were home ok."

"Well, I am…is there anything else?"

"…no. Bye Noel"

"Bye." I didn't get any sleep that night for worrying. Worrying about what the future held for us, about how I got to this point in my life and how I was going to go on without Noel, if I needed to do so; and equally as important, how I was going to go on *with* her. In my tossing and turning, I realized that for the first time since we started dating, I was close to not having Noel in my life and the thought petrified me.

My life had become extremely complicated in a matter of months and I stood at a crossroad. I tossed and turned in bed as I contemplated how to reconcile *being in love with a woman totally and completely, while still having incredibly strong cravings for the touch of a man.* And how to deal with the fact that even though this is most fulfilling relationship I've ever had, I can't tell anyone about it. I pride myself on not letting the attitudes of others dictate who I am or what I do, but let's be real, people don't want to hear about someone who's sexually confused. I didn't. And no matter how much I'd like to think that my *real* friends will be with me no matter what, I know I can only count on people to be human. After all, admitting to my relationship to my two best friends had proven that and destroyed our friendships in the process. So, as I saw it, my choices were to get out of the relationship and be miserable or to stay in it, not be able to open acknowledge it and consequently, be miserable. I got no sleep.

I still hadn't gotten any rest by the time that Christmas dinner rolled around and I guess that that's why my better judgment failed me. It had been six days since our argument and I still hadn't talked with Noel. I didn't have the energy to explain the absence of the big surprise that I had promised in anticipation of my *coming out*, so I asked Maurice to fill in for Noel. Of course, everyone just assumed that my surprise was that Moe and I are seeing each other. I must say, he did a great job staying in character, and he got along so well with my family that if one didn't know better they might think that I was the guest at his family gathering. Everybody complimented me on *my new man* in private, but as I sat cornered by my twenty something year-old tack-head niece, Joyce, I was beginning to have my doubts that bringing him was a good idea.

The men and women had adjourned to their separate holiday activities at this point. The women sat and talked or played board games with the children and the men watched football. I had been looking out the window deep in my own thoughts and quietly feeling guilty, while trying to convince myself that Maurice's presence and my consequent betrayal of Noel wasn't all that bad. I ignored

131

Joyce as best I could, until her comments broke my concentration.

"Guuuurl, he is fine. I bet you he be putting that shit down too! Damn! *And* he look like he packin' too. I bet that nigga can work a..."

"Joyce! Do you mind?"

"What?! Shoot I'm just saying what everybody else it thinking. Come on now guuurl, give up the tapes...is the dick good or what?"

"Go away Joyce."

"Damn! You ain't got to get all stuck up and shit! I'm just asking if your man can handle *his*."

"Whether or not *my* man can *handle his* is so not your business...so like I said, bye Joyce."

"Well, dang, you ain't got to be rude. Shit! I was just wondering if he had a brother or a friend or some shit, if he handlin' things. I jus' ain't trying to get with no weak niggas, though. Ya na' I'm sayin'. I needs me a solider and I'm just sayin', if he got a friend that know his way around the pussy, put a bitch down." *Oh my DAMN! I can't stand her ghetto ass.* If there is one thing I absolutely abhor even more than the word *nigga*, it's sisters that refer to themselves as *bitches*. I really shouldn't blame her though, cause she got every bit of her crudeness honestly. I mean, after all she is the child of my daddy's brother Uncle Snooky and his wife Aunt Gina. They are just about as country fabulous as one could ever get. At one point, a few years ago, when I was a little younger and less tolerant of foolishness, I went to both of them on separate occasions to find out what they thought about the way Joyce chooses to express herself verbally. I got, "I can't tell the little bitch nothin', she don't' listen to me none no way" from Aunt Gina." At this point, I figured somebody had to be the

132

voice of reason in all of this, but why I thought it might be Uncle Snooky, I don't know. I still shake my head every time I think of his grinning toothless words of wisdom on the subject, "well…you know Shay, it's like this here…in life they is two kinds of a woman. They is ladies and they is bitches and when it come to Joyce and Gina, you know I loves 'em dearly, but them bitches ain't no ladies." It was at that moment that I learned to mind my business and just try to peacefully co-exist with idiocy from afar when necessary.

"Good-bye-Joyce!" I looked her directly in the eye and enunciated the words very clearly, so that there was no misunderstanding my point. Apparently, she understood as she walked away rolling her eyes and mumbling something about me being a *stuck up hoe.*

"Don't take none of this shit personally, its just comedy." That was Tom as he walked over to me with drinks in both hands.

"Hey big head. Is that for me?" I asked, pointing to the drink in his left hand.

"Uh, no. It's actually for your boy Moe. It's half time and I'm on a drink run."

"Oh. So what do you think?" I don't know why I asked that question. I guess I got caught up in the pretend boyfriend moment.

"Oh, he's good peeps even though he is a Cowboys fan." I had always put a lot of store in what Tom thought of my boyfriends, because he was usually an excellent judge of character.

"But yo, I been meaning to ask, what's up with your girl Rachel? I saw her in the club a few days ago looking like she was *workin' the place.*"

"What you mean *workin' the place?*"

"I mean she was wearing boots that came to about mid thigh and a skirt that didn't quite come down that far."

"You saw her in the booty club?"

"Naw, in the regular club. Chrome in Philly."

"Seriously? You saw Rae Rae in Chrome looking like a hoochie?" I asked the question more out of shock than anything. I knew Tom was serious about what he had said. He knew how close Rachel and I were and about all of our history, except for our most recent tiff. Of all my friends Rachel was one of the few that he actually liked and could stand being around.

"Seriously. And I think I saw her leave with a dude and come back, without him, about an hour later. And isn't this around the time of her mom and her aunt's..."

"Yeah, it is..." I said cutting him off. We hadn't spoken in about five months and I had heard that she got fired for not showing up at work, but the thought that Rae Rae might have fell off and went back to using sex and or drugs as a crutch, hurt me. Even though she was the cause of our not being friends, I had promised to be there for her.

"Don't y'all usually spend the holidays together...how come she didn't come by."

"It's complicated." I wanted to talk to Tom, but to explain about Rachel would have meant having to explain about Noel. I had planned on telling Tom about Noel and I, before I told anybody else, *if* I told anybody else. But I was just not up to it at that moment. I had wanted to call Rachel many times in the past few weeks but again my pride had always stopped me. But now that I knew what was going on with her, pride or no pride, I just couldn't let her go out like that. At that moment, I decided that I was going to be true to my promise to be there for Rachel, whether she wanted me too or not. I just couldn't see myself turning

134

away from her when I knew she needed me. The ironic thing is that I felt like she did that exact thing to me when she walked out of the apartment that day. But be that as it may, my friendship is just not going to be conditional like that. Tom snapped me out of my thoughts.

"You alright?"

"Yeah…yeah, I'm fine. I'ma get Maurice and we're gonna stop by her spot on the way home."

"Y'all not leaving now are y'all?"

"Um hum…you just want somebody your age to watch the rest of the game with."

"And to provide a buffer from Snaggletooth Snooky. I ain't never met a man that used more words to describe less, in my whole life. And the man's breath ain't got to be that foul, I mean for real though." We both had to laugh at that one.

"I thought it was *just comedy*."

"Yeah…well…it is when you ain't dealing with it directly and having to have his drunk behind whisper damn near everything to, you *man to man*. And it's always shit that requires a lot of "h's" and "p's". I mean, damn Snooky!."

I had a good long talk with my dad while, Moe finished watching the game and we made our exit at about 9:15pm.

Again Never

It was about ten o'clock when Maurice and I got to
Rachel's house. I didn't know what to expect, but I could
barely control the gasp that threatened to escape from my
throat when I saw her. I had always seen Rachel as a
naturally beautiful woman, but I didn't recognize the
hideous creature standing in front of me. She looked
gaunt. I estimated that she had lost about 15-20 pounds,
which was not a good look for her when you consider that
she was only about a hundred and twenty pounds to start.
Her eyes looked sunken and like she hadn't had sleep in
years. To say that her hair was disheveled would be a step
up from what it was at the moment. Her lips looked dry
and cracked and there was a bruise that looked to be
healing under her right eye. She wore a pretty blue silk
paisley robe which smelled like it had not been washed in
few weeks too many. She had dirt under her nails and was
obviously embarrassed by her appearance as she cinched
the robe tighter and tried to smooth her hair down with the
other hand.

"What you doin' here?" were her first words to me as she
tried to ignore Maurice.

"I came to see you. We need to talk."

"We ain't got nothing to talk about Shay. I don't have
anything to say to you that I didn't say before. Besides,
I'm busy!"

"Yeah, well you can just listen then!"

"Shay, I don't wanna hear…" I had put my foot in the
doorway, in case she got any ideas about closing it.

"Look Rae Rae we can have this conversation out here in
earshot of all your neighbors, or we can go inside and talk

about it like civilized adults…whichever one you want. But we *are* having this conversation." I almost changed my mind as I entered the apartment. It turns out that it wasn't just funk that I was smelling, but a mixture of B.O., cigarettes, cheap perfume, marijuana and some other odor that I couldn't quite place. The place was a wreck and had empty alcohol bottles lying around, pizza boxes were strewn about, and other various empty wrappers and debris were littered throughout her apartment. Although, Maurice didn't say anything, I'm sure he must have been wondering what the hell I had gotten him into.

"Ok, you're in…talk."

"First of all it's not going to be that kind of conversation. You're not going to be dictating when it begins and ends."

"Shay, I don't know who the fuck you think…"

"AND SECOND, YOU STINK!!! I mean, like DAMN! So, before we do *any* talking at all, you are taking a bath." My emotions were going a mile a minute and I had gone from feeling sorry for her to being mad with myself for letting her down, and finally to being mad at her for allowing herself to come to such a pass. At this point, I was all up in her face and if she would have made just one move toward anyplace but the bathroom we would have been rolling all around her filthy apartment. Thank God she didn't and headed directly to the bathroom. I was relieved when I heard the water running for a bath, cause a shower just wasn't gon' get it at that point.

I asked Maurice to help me pick up the apartment while Rachel bathed, which he did graciously. When we were done I mentioned that he didn't have to stay and that I would be ok crashing at Rachel's place for the night, but he wouldn't hear of it.

"Naw, it's cool. I don't mind being here. I am glad you made her take a bath first though, cause Ohoo Woo…she look like she used to be fine, but that crack ain't no joke."

"Crack?"

"Yeah. You don't smell it. It's mixed in with all kinds of other stuff, but there's no mistaking that smell. My cousin Jennimae got hooked a few years ago and she ain't been right since…Anyway, I'll tell you what, why don't I leave y'all alone to talk for a couple of hours. You call me when you're ready to go, and I'll come get you."

"No, Maurice I couldn't ask you to do that. You've already given up your holiday to be with me and my crazy family. I couldn't ask…" Maurice put a finger to my lips to silence me.

"You didn't ask, I offered and I ain't trying to hear no. So, call me when you're ready to go, else I'll be back in about two hours."

"You know, you are such a wonderful man."

"Tell me something that I don't already know."

"Alright, Morris." I said as Maurice pretended to smooth his hair.

"Yeah, well you know it should have been Maurice Day and the Time."

"Ok. But you have to let me make it up to you."

"I can think of a few ways for that to happen."

"You ain't getting no freaky two for one either, so don't even think about it." We both laughed.

"Alright, well, not that I was thinking about that, but we'll figure something out."

"Um hum, indeed we will. I'll call you about 12:30 ok?"

"Well, why don't I just meet you back here at around that time, unless you need me sooner?"

"OK" I hugged Maurice tighter and longer than I meant

138

too. I could feel his package begin to bulge as we pulled apart and I don't know why but instead of letting him go, I kissed him. A deep, slow, passionate, either-we-got-to-stop-now-or-something-got-to-happen kind of kiss. And my body tingled as he walked out of the door.

We had done an excellent job of cleaning Rachel's apartment, if I did say so myself and I was lost somewhere between my reverie about the kiss Maurice and I had had and feeling guilty about having cheated on Noel, when Rachel's voice snapped me out of my thoughts.

"Alright...now, what is it?" Rachel was standing behind the couch wearing clean sweats, with her hair wrapped in a towel and her arms folded across her chest. Now she looked more like the Rachel I knew. She looked much more like my best friend then some crackhead. The thought was sobering as I thought about what Maurice had said and began to remember the odor that I couldn't place, from the druggies that came to the hospital.
"Rachel, what are you doing to yourself?"
"Minding my own damn business...why you trying to mind it too?"
"Because I care about you Rachel."
"Um hum...you *care* about me or do you want to get with me?" That hurt and if I wasn't sure that it was the drugs and the hurt talking, I would have either punched her in the face or been out...for good. But I did neither.
"Rachel, you're my best friend and I love you and I don't want to see anything bad happen to you."
"Yeah, well where were you a couple of weeks ago?"
"You told me that you weren't sure you wanted to be friends anymore, a couple of months ago remember?"

"So what, a true friend would have been there anyway."

"I am a true friend and that's why I'm here, even while you're insulting me and questioning my motives. I *am* your friend. I accept you for, and in spite of, who you are…"

"And I'm just supposed to accept that you're a cunt-licking…"

"And you're bitchy, crackhead, junkie, slut at the moment…but Rachel, I don't love you any less for it. You're my best friend. I see what you're doing to yourself and I just can't sit back and watch."

"Yeah, well, thank you but I'm alright."

"Rachel, you're not alright and that's why I'm here. We once promised that we wouldn't let each other be *not alright*…and, I'm here for you Rachel." I glanced down at my watch when I heard the doorbell ring. It was only a little after 10:45 so, I knew it wasn't Maurice coming back. Rachel looked a little nervous as she headed toward the door. I could hear the man on the other side of the door trying not to talk to loudly.

"…well, what you mean? You said ten thirty-ish and I needs me some ass tonight! C'mon girl you gots to *rock me tonight, for old time sake.*" The thought that this slimy little worm of a man had the nerve to even approach Rachel was enough to repulse me, but that he had likely used her body for his pleasure on other occasions absolutely incensed me.

"Excuse me dick-head, but what are you not getting here! She said no…ain't gon' be no *rockin'* tonight or any other night, so get the hell on…ya toad! 'The fuck is your problem!" I could tell he was scared, but he stood there trying to stare me down and if Rachel hadn't spoke up when she did, that would have been his ass.

"Do you mind… I can handle this." That was directed to me.

"Well, handle it then!"

"Look, Charles I can't tonight. My friend's got a problem and I need to talk to her about it."

"Yeah, Chuck, not tonight!! She can't tonight!! Get the fuck out Chuck!! Bye-Bye and Don't ever come back, Chuck!!"

"Well, if not tonight when then?" He was a persistent little blob of a man.

"Never! Chuck!! Now take your pudgy, little, sawed off, perverted, ass and get the fuck!!"

"Now, hold up. That bitch ain't got no call to be talking to me like that."

"Bitch!!!??" Rachel and I said in unison.

"Hold the fuck up, that's my best friend you're talking about and if you ever fix your mouth to call her that shit again. I will fuck-you-up!! Now, you need to leave my motherfuckin' house." And judging by the way Chuck turned on his heals and got out of dodge, he knew that she meant every single word. Now that was the Rachel I knew.

"Damn! Your scrawny little ass almost scared me." It felt good to share a laugh with my best friend again.

"Look, Shay your being with Noel scares me, because I don't want to loose you."

"You're not gonna loose me, I'm always gon' be here for you."

"I guess I know that, but for so long it's just been me and you. You know I can't get with the girl on girl stuff…but if it's what makes you happy, I will try to be tolerant. I would have said that that night, but you had lied to me about Richard and then I found out about Noel the way I did. Shay you are my girl…my ace boon-coon…and I just

141

can't imagine anybody being closer to me than you and I guess I always imagined that it to be the same way with you. But when Noel came into the picture, all that changed for me. In my mind, she was gon' be the close one and I was gon' be on the outside looking in... I guess I was jealous of her in some ways."

"Rachel, you know better than that. You are like the sister I never had and nothing could ever come between us. And nothing is going to take away from our closeness, not a man, not a woman, nothing." I hugged Rachel and we both cried for a few minutes.

"Shay, I'm sorry for the way I've acted. Let it be said from this point on, I don't care who you date, I just don't want you to ever stop being my friend, again. I love you...punani breath.."

"I told you, we are girls for life and love you too...stank hoe." We talked for a little while before Maurice came back trying to figure out how to get Rachel back on track. It turns out that she hadn't got fired, but had taken an unpaid leave of absence and although she wasn't exactly trickin' she had lowered her standards by about a mile and was dating/sexin' a lot a guys that didn't care anything about her, but kept her supplied with Marijuana. The one guy, Charles whom we had just run off, introduced her to crack cocaine earlier this evening, which, thank God, she said she hated. That explained everything but the bruise under her eye, but I wasn't exactly in the mood to pry just yet.

Maurice was true to his word and got back at exactly 12:30. On the way home I played with the idea of Moe staying the night, but my conscious wouldn't let me do it. I was already feeling guilty on a whole lot of levels and I

142

couldn't add anymore to it. Well, maybe just a little more, which came in the way of another kiss at my door. This one was just as passionate as the first one and I really, really wanted him, but I just couldn't bring myself to do it. "…umph, Maurice I really like doing that with you and as much as I want you to stay, I love Noel and it just wouldn't be right. So we'd better call it a night, before I rip your clothes off and attack you right here."

"Yeah…nobody wants that" Maurice said as he moved closer to me. We kissed for another few minutes, before I broke it up again.

"You say that, but your body doesn't seem to be in agreement."

"That's only because I'm lying." Maurice said as we kissed and grinded in the hallway of my building. And finally, when he couldn't take it anymore, Maurice said

"Alright, I really do have to go. Cause if I don't…let's just say it's going to be an uncomfortable ride home."

"OK. Call me when you get in?" I relented.

"I will."

"Bye." I said sweetly as I watched him walk back toward his car.

I was exhausted, but I stayed up waiting for Maurice's call. When the phone rang twenty minutes later, I was thankful.

"Hey, you home?"

"Yeah, I'm home!" The female voice at the other end of the phone was not pleasant and certainly was not Maurice.

"Noel? Hey, I wasn't expecting you."

"I know you weren't…you were probably expecting your little boy toy. You know, I only asked for one thing from this relationship and that was for you to be honest about your feelings for me and you couldn't even do that. Just to

143

be honest, but you couldn't even…at first I thought that you were just some straight chick who was curious, but then I really did start to believe that things could be different with you, but there you were making out like some horny school girl with your *just a friend*…you are so foul. I wish I did have some other words to explain how much you hurt me, but I don't. So seeing as how I don't have anymore words, goodbye Shelita. "

"Wait, Noel, don't hang…hello…shit!" I tried to call Noel back for three hours straight, but got a busy signal every time. By six o'clock the next morning I had not gotten any sleep and my eyes were red and puffy from crying and I had made up my mind that Noel was just too important to me to let her go without a fight. So I tucked my pride neatly in my pocket and got myself together, showered and was at her door by 8:00am.

I could hear Stephanie's voice asking Noel what she wanted her to do as I knocked on the door. Apparently she told her to let me in as the door opened slowly.

"Noel, I'm so sorry…I never meant to hurt you…" I cut my eyes at Stephanie for her non-verbal disbelieving commentary.

"Does she have to be here?"

"I'm not the problem here. It's about your confusion, that's what's at issue."

"Whatever the fuck the issue is, it doesn't concern you, so could you please excuse yourself." I stepped in Stephanie's direction.

"No, Shelita she can stay. Steph is right. Just say what you have to say."

"Fine. Noel, I do still crave the touch of a man sometimes and that's all that was last night. I didn't realize, how much

144

I did and I 'm sorry you had to see what you saw; but what you didn't see was me tell him that it couldn't go any further because I'm in love with you. And besides you said, if I ever had the need…"

"I know what I said! And I know what you said in response…and you're right I didn't see any of that last part. What I did see was my lover being held and kissed by someone else in public for everyone who might walk by, to see. And it doesn't matter if it was a male or a female, it hurt all the same. It's one thing for me to know about it, but not have to be exposed to it. But, do you know what it's like to actually *see* you lover kissing someone else…well, let me show you. Stephanie can I borrow you lips for a minute." I could not believe what I was seeing and I didn't know what shocked me more. I wasn't sure if I was more taken aback by the fact that Noel kissed Stephanie or that Stephanie had actually let herself be kissed like that, knowing that it was only for my benefit. In any event, I was livid.

"Noel why would you do that…I mean, you just gon' kiss this bitch right in front of me." Stephanie started to respond to my calling her a bitch, but the look on my face told her not to dare, and she didn't.

"I'm just showing you what I saw."

"No you weren't. Because what *you* saw was my frailty as a human being, my struggle with trying to do the right thing by us, which I admit, was getting the best of me at the time. What *I* just saw was you being intentionally hurtful, vindictive, thoughtless, callous, disrespectful, cold, unfeeling, I could go on…but I'm not. Your only goal with what you just did was to hurt me…well…you did. I hope you're happy." Though I tried with all my might, I couldn't stop the tears from falling as I stormed out of

145

Noel's home and quite possibly her life.

Daddy's Home

"Look, it's gonna hurt for a while…" after three straight weeks of listening to me cry and whine about Noel, our relationship and her pleas of *sorrow* and of wanting to get me back, Moe had turned out to be a better friend than I imagined he would. He was always very patient with me and never tried to rush the healing process. I knew he wanted to be more than my friend, but he never pushed the issue and he was always right there.

"…but eventually you'll be ok. Give yourself a chance to heal. You can't rush the process."

"I know, but I just want the pain to stop. I think about her everyday and it doesn't help that she calls me just about everyday trying to get back together." I had told Maurice that I was ready to start dating him if he still wanted to see me, primarily because I wanted to get beyond the pain I was feeling, by filling up the void with something else. But he was patient.

"Look, sometimes you just have to let it hurt. I guarantee you that you'll know what to do when the time comes. So, just give yourself some time. We both know, it's not a good idea for us to start dating right now. I mean, I want you…goodness knows, I want you, but I want you to want *me* for the right reasons. I can't believe I'm even saying that. I mean, as recent as six months ago my ex-fiancée told me that I was a selfish fool that didn't know a damned thing about love and that my only redeeming quality was that I ate a mean coochie. Well…I'm paraphrasing but that was the gist of it.

"Well, I think she was wrong. I don't think you're selfish at all…I have to say, I *am* interested in finding out about

the coochie eating part, but you don't seem selfish to me."
We both laughed a good hearty laugh and for the first time
in a long time, as we said our goodbyes hung up the phone,
I felt just a little lighter.

When the phone rang again at two o'clock the next
morning I assumed that it was Noel telling me how sorry
she was for the millionth time, but I was surprised to hear
my dad on the other end.
"…daddy? What's wrong?"
"Baby girl, your Nanna's in the hospital. Tom's on his way
over to get you."
"Oh, my God…is she gonna be alright?"
"Well, they say that it was mild stroke, but they're worried
about her heart at this point."
"Oh my God…alright, I think that's Tom at the door, I'm
gon' throw something on and I'll see y'all soon." I had
dressed in under 30 seconds and was ready to go when I
flung the door open. To my surprise, though, it wasn't
Tom, but Noel.
"Look, Noel I don't have time for this right now. My
grandmother is in the hospital and I'm waiting…" Before I
could get out the rest of the words Tom came hurriedly
around the corner.
"Hey, did dad call you?"
"Yeah, he told me. Is she alright?"
"They don't really know, so we need to get on down there."
"Alright, I'm ready. Let's go."
"Y'all mind if I come along too." Tom had met Noel
before, as *a good friend of mine*, and spoke before I had a
chance to respond.
"Naw, we don't mind. But we need to be out, now." I was
not in the mood to argue, so I let it go.

148

I stared blankly out of the window of the front seat of Tom's Cavalier as we headed toward the hospital. Noel finally got the hint and stopped trying to make conversation when I when I stopped responding to her chatter at all. I was still wounded by the thought of that day at her house with Stephanie and I was not about to just forget it, simply to spare her feelings. Besides there was another aspect to consider at this point. I just couldn't let this be about her, not right now…not when I needed to be focusing on my own pain and what I would do if Nanna ...

What I really needed was a friend to be there with me through this, so I called one.

"Hey…no…I'm on my way to the hospital…no nothing like that." I rolled my eyes and put a finger to my other ear to block out the look of hurt on Noel's face and the noise of her unspoken questions that were resonating in my ear. Nonetheless, I continued my conversation.

"… Nanna had a stroke…they're worried about her heart…yeah, I'm ok I guess. You think you could meet me at the hospital? OK…I'll see you there. Bye." As I went back to staring out of the window, I could see Noel silently wipe tears from her face from my periphery, but this was not about her.

Nanna was resting when we got to the hospital and so they wouldn't allow us to see her at that point, but they told us that the doctor would come out and tell us about Nanna prognosis shortly. Unfortunately, *shortly* didn't occur until an hour and fifteen minutes later. Noel had used the first twenty minutes of that time holding my hand and comforting me and pleading for my forgiveness every time we were out of earshot of my family members. Fortunately for her, my parents and Tom had gone to the cafeteria.

Unfortunately for me, she wouldn't stop until I confronted her about it directly.

"Noel, now is really not the time or the place for this…I can't deal with *this* and you at the same time. When did you become so selfish? Nanna almost died today…ok, she almost died! And all you can think about is what you need to say to get back in good with me?!" Even though, at this point I was more irritated than anything, I felt a tinge of sadness for Noel as she began to look like a child scolded by her parents.

"…you're right Shay, but I've just been so miserable and I don't know what I can do to reach you…" Her tears had already started to flow as she was talking, but turned into all out sobs as Maurice brushed by her and took me into his arms. Noel hurriedly picked up her coat and rushed out of the door. My mind was spinning at this point. Part of me wanted to go after and comfort her, but the part that was in control of my ambulating through space and time said *damn that, I ain't goin no damned where.* I hate to admit it, but I guess deep down I was happy that Noel was leaving my life. I needed some normalcy. I was tired of hiding what I felt for my lover from my family and tired of quietly feeling ashamed of what and who I'd become. And…it felt good to have Maurice's strong arms around me. I felt secure. Unfortunately, my mind wouldn't let the image of the hurt look on Noel's face leave me until Maurice's words finally barged in on my thoughts.

"Are you alright?" I gently wept as I nodded my head against his chest.

"Have you heard anything about your grandma yet?" Maurice's question reminded me that I had not really heard anything new since arriving at the hospital.

Just as I finished updating him on Nanna's situation, her doctor finally came to talk to us. Mom and dad had been praying together and Tom was in his own little world, until Dr. Phillips began to give us a play by play. He explained the term Transient Ischemic Attack (TIA) which is just doctor mumbo jumbo for a mild stroke. I knew most of what he was telling us already, but I listened intently anyway. Dr. Phillips explained to the family that TIA's are caused by a temporary lack of oxygen to the brain that does not cause permanent damage and that, because Nanna's was caught and treated early, a full blown stroke is not very likely at this point. He finished by saying that there is still some concern about Nanna's preexisting heart condition, but that even that seems to be stable and is not a huge concern at this point. Before he left, Dr. Phillips said that we could see Nanna as soon as she was awake. It took some doing, but I was able to convince everyone else to go home to get some rest and come back first thing in the morning. As for me I was going to pull up a chair next to Nanna's bed and make camp for the night.

Maurice sat with me holding my hand the whole while, until even he had to admit that the rumbling sound coming from his throat was not exactly typical of a man who was only *resting [his] eyes.* It took some convincing, but he finally gave in, kissed me lightly and promised to come back first thing in the morning.

At last I was alone with Nanna and I couldn't help but reminisce to myself about all of the wonderful times that I had had with her and Gramps as I was growing up. I didn't realize I had said anything out loud until I was almost startled to hear my own voice saying *life seemed so much simpler then.*

151

"Life always seems simple when you're not pretending to be something you're not."

"Nanna, you're awake!"

"You think I don't know that child? I been 'wake for the better part of an hour now, listening to you and that young man that was in here with you –snoring louder than a broken buzz saw."

"I'm sorry Nanna. We didn't mean to wake you."

"Well, no harms a foul chile'." I had corrected Nanna a million times about this cliché in particular, but it was music to my ears at this point.

"I was so scared that I was gon' lose you, I just didn't know what to do. I love you so much Nanna and I don't know what I would do without you."

"You would go on living, chile. Now stop all that foolish talk. Dying is just part of the cycle, baby, and if the Good Lord decides it's my time, then that's what it is. But I got a little bit more in me, 'sides I got to help you get this raggedy life of yours in order."

"Mam?"

"Well what you gon' do now baby girl?"

"Mam?"

"I say, what you gon' do now?"

"About what Nanna?"

"About this crazy life of yours…one minute you in love with this one, the next you're with that one...I'm exhausted just trying to keep track."

"Mam?"

"Don't you keep '*mam-ing*' me chile'. I'm talking about the girl we had dinner with a few months ago and the buzz-saw man that just left here. If there's one thing Mama know it's when her child is in love. You can try to hide it as much as you want, but Mama know. I see'd the way she look at you and the way you looked at her for that matter. Chile' Stevie Wonder would've knowd, she was more than just your friend, even if I hadn't seent you stealing touches and kisses when you thought I wasn't looking. Mama know baby." I was shocked to hear my Nanna telling that she knew about Noel, and I didn't know what to do. I was embarrassed and I didn't know what to say next. Sensing my uneasiness, Nanna continued

"…and baby, if there is one thing that I thought I would have taught you by now, it's that there is nothing in this world that you can do to make me stop loving you. And baby that's what you need to realize. Ain't nobody in this world gon' gives you they approval, if you don't give it to yourself first. God made you just as wonderfully goofed up as you are, and chile you ain't got no call to let nobody make ya feel shame 'bout that. I know you and I love because of it and 'times, in spite of it. I don't know why you felt like you had to hide this thing, but since you did, I decided to let you come to me in your own time. But baby, the truth is, I don't know how much time I have left…"

"Oh Nanna don't say that…"

"Well, it's true baby. None of us do. And now I see you with this young man and I just don't know what to think and by the look on your face it must be confusing to you too."

"Nanna I wanted to come to you with it, but I didn't want to stress you out and I just didn't know what to do. I didn't know how you would react and I didn't want to worry you."

"Lord-have-mercy child, hush your fuss!" Nanna's voice was weak and punctuated with a coughing spell.

"Did I do something, make ya think you couldn't talk to me." Nanna's voice was more accusatory than questioning.

153

"No, no, no, you've always been there for me Nanna, but this just felt different. I don't know...people get funny when you start talking about sexual preference and they get judgmental."

"Chile, the only judgment you have to worry about is the Lord's and don't nobody else's matter. Seek out the Lord's voice baby."

"Nanna, I did...and I just wound up in a cult-like religious sect that wanted to marry me and a bunch of other women off to the same man."

"No, baby...you done went off all half cocked, flying off the handle looking for the cliff notes to what God is trying to tell you, but that's not how He works sweetie. The church and church folk don't always have anything to do with the Lord. What you need to do is to try to listen to that voice down in your soul. Our flesh can monk things up, sometimes, but your soul come from the Lord, Chile'. That's the voice you need to hear and take heed to."

"Sometimes it's hard to do that Nanna..."

"Well, who said it's gonna' be easy chile'. Nobody promised you a rose garden. The key to life is to get in touch with that voice. That's gonna' help you figure out when the things in your life require action and when they requires you to be still."

"But..."

"But nothing child. I knows you feel like you have to be moving and doing all the time, but baby sometimes you just have to be still. If you do, I guarantee you that God will tell you where he wants you to be...and you'll be a lot happier and a lot better off. Now what is it with these people, you pussyfootin' 'round wit'. Do any of 'em make ya happy?"

"I guess, Nanna. I mean, I've never felt for anybody, what

154

I feel for Noel. It's the strangest feeling I've ever had, because I need her and I want her and I love her so bad it hurts, but I'm also ashamed of her and of me when I'm with her; and sometime what she does just drives me crazy. On the other hand, there's Maurice and he's sweet and sensitive and I enjoy being around him, but I just don't feel as strongly about him as I do for Noel. She just provokes really strong emotion in me and....well to be honest Maurice is somebody that's cool to hang out with, but for some reason I just don't get the same feeling about him as I do Noel.."

"Well, baby, just know that God does everything for a reason and obviously you got something to learn from the both of them and you just got to figure out what you're supposed to take from your relationships with them."

"How do I figure that out Nanna?"

"I just told ya, you just listens for God's voice baby." I could tell that Nanna was tired and I was exhausted, so we left the conversation there and we both fell fast asleep. I laid down next to Nanna on the small uncomfortable hospital bed and had the most restful sleep of my life that night.

I had a new lease on life and for the first time in a long time I knew just what I wanted and needed to do. I felt like a load had been lifted and I was resolved as I knocked on Noel's door. I was tempted to wait for her to get back home when she didn't answer, but quickly thought better of it. The last thing I needed was to be caught off guard by any of Noel's actions at this point. I needed to stay focused. I nearly gasped when I turned and walked smack dab into Noel and Rennie walking arm in arm toward her apartment. I thought I saw Rennie quickly take her hand off Noel's ass as they uncoiled and continued their approach to my end of the hall. I was prepared to do what I had to do, but still the sight of them together made me uneasy and there I was, way off guard.

"Listen, I need to talk to you." I said, doing my best to ignore my one-time friend Rennie.

"Is that right? I would have thought you were too busy with your *just-a-friend* to be bothered with me."

"Look Noel, I'm not in the mood for games right now, OK? I just want...I just need to talk to you...and for the record I could say that *I would have thought that you would be too busy out getting revenge.* Oh, by the way *hi Rennie.*" I could tell the comment stung Rennie almost as much as Noel, but as far as I could see, it was true.

"Shay, I don't know who..." That was Rennie, but Noel stopped her tirade before she got started.

"Rennie baby she's right, we do need to talk. Do you think I could take a rain-check on the movie." *Movie...baby...did she just call her baby? What the fuck?!*

"Ok, so talk." That was Noel after having said goodbye to Rennie and let us into her apartment.

"Oooo-k, well first off I just want to say I'm sorry. That night at the hospital, I wasn't thinking clearly and the bottom line is that I didn't mean to throw anything in your face. I..."

"How is your grandmother?"

"She's doing ok. She didn't have any residual problems from the stroke. They say it was just a mild one."

"Well that's good...look, I don't want to step on your apology, but that was three weeks ago Shay. UM...where you been sis'?"

"I needed to figure some things out and I just needed some

156

time for myself."

"You couldn't have picked up the phone to say that? Look, I'm sorry Shay, but you hurt me and I'm not just talking about that time. Do you know what it's like to love someone so deeply that it hurts to think about living without them? And to have that person be ashamed of the love that you feel for them. Do you know what it's like to see your mate in another person's arms looking like they could not be more content?"

"No. But do you know what it's like to love someone more deeply than you ever thought that you could, yet to feel like shit because you just can't seem to give yourself completely over to the feeling, all while that person is pressuring you to get it together."

"Shay, I never pressured you."

"You have got to be kidding me! What about Thanksgiving and Christmas?"

"That was about me being tired of loving you 100% and not ever being acknowledged outside of the bedroom or of my circle of friends. And it's like you only did it there because you're afraid that someone else might, if you didn't."

"That's so not fair, Noel. I loved you with all my heart."

"Loved?"

"Love. I do love you Noel, like I've never loved anyone. But it's just not enough. Not anymore. I can't stand feeling guilty about being with you anymore."

"So, you would let what people might say, get in the way of our love?"

"It's not people I'm worried about."

"Well, what then?"

"It's a lot of things. But mostly, it's me. It's coming to terms with who I am today and why I'm doing what I'm doing. It's about finding out about what I want out of life and more importantly about finding out what God wants from me in my life."

"God?" It was hard to believe, but in the 11and ½ months that we had dated Noel, and I had never even discussed religion. We'd met right after my church fiasco and I guess it just never came up.

"Yes, God... You do believe in God, don't you?"

"Of course I do, but I also believe that God made me as I am. So, it offends me when you imply that..."

"Noel, I'm not implying anything. I'm just saying that even as good as it feels when I'm with you, this is not right for me. It's not what's right for *me*. I can't handle it. I'm sorry."

"Don't be. The one thing I've always asked for from you is that you be honest with me about how you feel. I can deal with your not being able to hang. Make no mistake, it hurts and I am disappointed and I am so very angry with you. But at the very least, now I can stop chasing something that's not going to happen. You know, the funny thing is that I knew, but I just kept on hoping that things would be different. I can *not* tell you how much it hurt me to have you let go of my hand because we were coming up on a group of people when we were out walking. Every time we were in that situation, I kept thinking to myself that maybe *this* will be the time that she holds on to me...holds on to us, but you never did. A little piece of me died every time you let go, but still *I* hoped for the best. I was never ashamed of you and there was nothing that I wouldn't say or do or *be* for you. There were times when I hated myself for that...I hated that your *love*...that your *approval* meant that much to me...that morning with Stephanie, I wanted you to feel just a little bit of the degradation that I

158

constantly felt, being in love with you." Tears were flowing down Noel's face as she spoke and I wanted her to stop talking, because every word cut me more deeply than the one before and I'd never been more ashamed of who I was, than at that moment. My whole life I'd wanted nothing more than for someone to love me unconditionally, and when I finally got it, I had treated her it like it was nothing. I was incapable of giving her that same thing in return. Even though I had gone there to break off the relationship, the finality of actually doing it gored me more deeply that I had even imagined. At this point, my own tears were flowing and I wanted to comfort Noel, but she stopped me as I approached her.

"Please don't. I didn't tell you that to get your pity or sympathy. I just want you to understand what you had in me." My voice broke as I began to speak

"…and I'm not standing here because I pity you. Noel, I just want you to know that I really do love you with all that I am…and I need, right now, for you to know that I am so sorry for the way I've treated you and this relationship. I don't disapprove of you, I…" Noel stopped my words.

"I'm sorry too. But unfortunately, it doesn't matter at this point. Can you please leave now?!" I had gone to Noel's apartment for the express purpose of ending our relationship, because a nagging feeling in my soul told me that our being together was wrong. But now that I had, I wondered if the voice inside me wasn't wrong. My mind raced over the many different bad relationship decisions that I've made in the past, as I considered that I had just given up someone who loved everything about me and was willing to brazenly declare it before all the world, someone who was willing to learn everything I had to teach, someone who knew my shortcomings and yet was

159

unmoved. And I had given it all up, because society, some in my family, and as far as I could tell, *my voice*, said she was the wrong gender.

When a person loves a woman

Tears blurred my vision as I drove around aimlessly, trying to understand my feelings and how I was going to get on with my life without Noel. I had rehearsed what I would say to her a thousand times and the outcome had turned out to be ultimately exactly what I planned. Yet I still hurt. My stomach churned, nausea threatened to overtake me as I drove and my tears often made it difficult to see the road. I finally wound up at Maurice's house. I don't exactly know why I went there, but I didn't want to be alone.

Maurice and I had become closer over the past few weeks and I felt safe with him. He had expressed an interest in dating and honestly, I guess that that's where we were headed from the start. However, I needed to sort things out with Noel and I wasn't really ready to entertain that idea just yet. I glanced in the mirror as I got off the elevator to Moe's floor and tried to fix myself up a little. My eyes were a little puffy and red from crying, but I don't think anyone else would have noticed. It dawned on me that I hadn't called as I approach his door and suddenly this didn't seem like such a good idea anymore. Before I could turn completely around, Moe's door opened. There was feminine giggling as a woman playfully stepped back into the hallway. She was about two inches taller than me and very pretty. A shirtless Maurice grabbed at her waist pleading with her to stay a little while longer. They seemed to notice me at the same time and Maurice straightened up like a child with his hand in the cookie jar, cleared his throat and tried to be nonchalant.
"Ooooh, Um…hey…Lita…um…what…what…what you doing here?" *Wanting to crawl under a rock,* was my

silent response.

"I…uh, I was just passing by the neighborhood and figured I'd stop in a say hi." *Ms. Pretty* was beginning to look a little annoyed and cleared her throat to give voice to it in no uncertain terms.

"Oh…damn. Jacqueline this is…"

"Just a friend!" My words were louder than I intended and overlapped Maurice's mention of my name, which I repeated as I extended my hand.

"Shelita."

"Nice to meet you."

"Yeah, same here. But listen this was a bad idea, I've got a really bad habit of not calling before I stop by…so, I'm…I didn't mean to interrupt anything…I'm gon' just be on my way."

"OK, bye-bye then." That was *Pretty* again and under normal circumstances, that would have gotten a rise out of me, but I just didn't have anymore fight in me. As I turned to walk away, I could hear the hushed argument between she and Maurice going on behind me.

While sitting in the comfort of my car, again the tears fell freely and my vision was blurred the entire way home. It was only by the grace of God that I didn't get into an accident. Of course the first thing I saw when I had eased out of my clothes and into bed was the framed picture-poem that Noel had written and given to me on my birthday. *When you're not near, I gather my most cherished memories of you, as though they were garments lightly scented with the sweet fragrance of your skin, and revel in epicurean thought as I wrap myself in every stitch of each sweet remembrance.* I've never felt the kind of pain I felt that moment. I ignored the phone, which must

162

have rang a hundred times before I finally took it off the hook and cried myself to sleep clutching the picture and trying to hold on to my last little bit of sanity.

When I checked the machine in the morning there were 10 messages. Two of the messages were from Maurice apologizing and wanting to explain about Jacqueline, another two were hang ups that I suspect were from him as well, three were from Noel wanting to find out if I made it home alright, two were from Rachel saying that she just had a weird feeling and was concerned about me, and the one I really didn't expect was from Rennie. I had to play it twice just to make sure I heard right. *Hello, Shelita...look, I know it's been a long time and...I'm sorry we ran into each other like we did last night...and I just want to say...look, I would much rather do this in person or at the very least, I'd like to be able to hear your voice. Please call me when you get the message.* I barely had a chance to digest all of the messages when I heard a knock at the door. I was surprised, but pleasantly so, to see the one friend I had left standing there at the door when I looked out.

"C'mon now it's cold out hure!" I stood behind the door as I let Rachel in.

"What's up g..." She stopped in mid-sentence as she caught sight of me.

"Baby, what is wrong?"

"Is it that obvious?"

"Well, yeah. You've got tears stains on your cheeks and your eyes are blood shot...are you alright?" And for the first time in too long, I allowed myself to fall apart and be comforted by my best friend. *My girl...for life.*

"Look, you could do way better than her anyway! If she doesn't understand what she had in you, then fuck her! And fuck him too for that matter! What I know is that time heals all wounds and you are going to be ok."

"How do you know that?"

"Because I ain't gon' let you not be ok, apple-head!"

Rachel sat and listened to my ranting for as long as I needed her to do so.

I felt so much better after talking with Rachel that I decided to meet with Rennie instead of calling. What I needed was closure and I was sure that a telephone conversation would have been much more awkward, since we hadn't spoken in months before running into each other last night.

"Hey…" There was a pregnant pause after Rennie's first word as though she were waiting for me to cuss her out. I didn't. Because even though I wanted to very badly for several reasons, I still wanted to know why she just had to talk to me.

"I'm here." I tried not to sound to cold.

"So you are. First, I want to say thank you for coming to talk to me. It's not like you had to or anything and I just…I appreciate it." She quickly moved on as, I guess, my face registered my irritation with her pending soliloquy. .

"…anyway, Shay I just want to say I'm sorry. I'm sorry for last night, but even more importantly I'm sorry for a few months ago. I wasn't upset with you, per se."

"Well, you fooled me, cause it sounded like I was the one."

"…Let me explain. A few weeks before I met Noel and introduced her to you and Rae Rae, I met a man. I mean, he was just something wonderful. I never thought I could feel that way for a man again, but I did and it scared me. So when I met Noel and she asked for my number I gave it

164

to her, but I couldn't bring myself to end the relationship with Terrance. That's why I couldn't commit to Noel and why things just got confusing…"

"Rennie what does all this have to do with me."

"Right. Well, the day you told me about you and Noel, Terrance and I had a big blowout. I found out I was pregnant and more than anything in the world I wanted to keep it and for Terrance to want me to keep it and for a second he did. Or at least it seemed like he did. We started talking about what we were going to do about a future and I just felt like he needed to know about my sexuality. I thought he would see how I felt about him and would say that it didn't matter, but he hit the roof. He wanted to know how, if I felt so strongly for him, I could cheat on him with Noel and I didn't really have a very good answer. All I could say was that I wanted to be sure about us. Unfortunately, that didn't make things any better and he started yelling about how confused and devoid of morals I was and about how I may have exposed him to "God only knows what diseases", and as he put it "some ole' gay shit". Anyway, he just wouldn't listen to reason and started talking about us breaking up and me getting "rid of the it" in reference to the baby. And that's where you came in. I had been crying all day and trying to figure out what I could say or do to get him back and you called saying that you wanted to start dating Noel. I felt like I was losing everything. Shay, you are one of my best friends and I don't want to lose you. I'm so sorry for the way I treated you." Rennie held out her arms as tears silently rolled down her face.

"I'm so sorry that you had to go through that and by yourself no less, but that doesn't explain everything Rennie. What you said, hurt me more than anybody's been

165

able to in quite some time. But, what about the other night? You knew what that Noel and I weren't done with each other at that point." Rennie apologized some more and went on to explain that she broke up with Terrance, but was going to keep the baby right up until she miscarried six weeks later. She explained that last night was the first time that she and Noel had seen each other since we had started dating and that they had both had a little too much to drink. She told me about how Noel couldn't stop talking about me and how one thing almost lead to another (my words not hers) as they ended up back at Noel's place. I genuinely felt bad for Rennie, but I still wasn't quite ready to commiserate with her.

"Rennie, like I said, I'm sorry you had to go through what you had to go through, I really am, but your friendship meant a lot to me and I needed you when I called you that night. I needed someone to understand how confused and miserable I was at that point in my life and maybe even offer a shoulder to lean on. And of all the people in the world who might have been able to understand exactly what I was going through, it should have been you. I mean, you knew first hand about the…" my voice trailed off as I remembered the confusion after the last conversation I had had with Rennie.

"…but not only could you not be there for me, but you made me feel like dirt. And even though I didn't know about everything that was going on in your life, it felt like you thought I was responsible for all of the misery that you were going through."

"I'm not going to lie to you Shay, at that point I did feel like it was your fault. I'm not saying it was right, but I felt like, if you hadn't slept with Thouron then maybe I might not be a single parent, struggling to raise my child and wouldn't have known anything about a lesbian lifestyle or any of the problems I was having at the time."

"Um…wow…part of me understands that I deserve that for sleeping with Thouron, but the other part thinks that it really stinks that you could throw it in my face. Through it all though, what you need to realize is that I didn't steal your husband. I had a physical relationship with him and when you got confirmation, you initiated the divorce. That was jacked up on my part, I know, but if he wasn't out looking for someone else in the first place, I couldn't have gotten with him. You yourself said that the marriage had been over for some time at that point. And in terms of your exploring an alternative life style, Rennie, one doesn't just *become* gay…"

"Why not Shay? You did. Remember?"

"Rennie, my situation was totally different and you know it…all, I'm saying is that the feelings you had were there long before I ever met Thouron, and you know that. And all our affair did was simply gave you an excuse to explore them and to get out of a bad marriage."

"I know that Shay…the point that I was trying to make was that *that* was my thought process at the time and that's why I treated you so badly."

"Well, I'm sorry but, as I said, that doesn't explain everything for me. You were one of my closet friends Rennie and you knew the kind of struggle that I've always had with trying to fit in somewhere…just trying to find a spot that felt comfortable in my own skin, you knew about everything that I was struggling with. And, yet all you could do was make me feel worse…and then for you to suggest that I would get with Rashan someday, that was just low."

"I know that Shay and I'm sorry, that's all I've been saying

167

since you walked through the door."

"I hear you Rennie, but I don't know if I can get over the things you said…and then add to that the fact that, I assume, that you and Noel may resume dating now…it's just too much for me to deal with."

"Shay, I think she could really be somebody special in my life and I want to explore that possibility, but if you don't want me too, I won't. Your friendship is more important to me than that."

"I appreciate that, but if that's true, exactly how important is having a relationship with her to you. And to follow that line of thought, if the relationship isn't all that important to you, why would you add insult to injury to our relationship, by dating her in the first place. …You know, of all the hurtful things you said to me on the day I told you about Noel and I, you said one thing that really resonated with me. And that was that I have had a tendency to make some piss poor decisions when it comes to relationships. Well, I'm trying to make better decisions about my relationships at this point, and truthfully, Rennie, I don't know if I can continue be friends with you."

I hadn't planned on saying any of those things to Rennie, but the more we talked, the more it just seemed right to just go our separate ways. I believe that some folks are only meant to be in our lives for a time and our time had probably just run it's course. I was serious about trying to make better relationship decisions in my life and it feels like I'm off to a pretty good start. Make no mistake, I hurt every time I think of being without Noel. Even so, something inside me just won't let me go back. I'd estimate that I had 98% of everything I ever thought I wanted in a relationship, with her, but if I'm honest with

168

myself, I have to admit that I need the rest in order to truly be happy and feel comfortable in my own skin. I'm trying to be ok with the fact that the beaten path, may not exactly be mine. But what I know for sure is that I'm not ok with settling for what's *good enough*, anymore. There's a nagging fear inside me that constantly reminds me that I may never find all that I'm looking for, but I take consolation in the fact that at least I will know that I never short changed myself or those that care about me.

If this experience has taught me anything, it's to never be ashamed of who I am or of the people that love me. My loved ones, quite simply, love me to the marrow, without question or condition, and without regard for what I have the potential to become. They love me not only for the woman *I am*, but also *in spite of her*. In any event, I need to end this because I have to get ready for a date. It turns out that *Miss Pretty*, Maurice's friend Jacqueline, is actually kind of cool. We bumped into each other, of all places, at work. It seems she's a social worker at a nearby rehab and had to accompany a patient to have his stomach pumped after he attempted to over dose on Tylenol. In any event, she apologized for being rude that day at Moe's apartment a few months ago and asked me out for a drink. So technically, it's not a *date* date, but just hanging out with someone who might become a good friend. And no, I'm not attracted to her...well not really. I mean, it's not like I *really* wanna get with her or anything...yet. Look, I know what I said about not being attracted to other women and it was true at the time that I said it, but the lessons that I've learned over the past year have quietly taught me that the place to call home, for which I've been searching all of my life, is not a place that even exists in the physical universe. That place, is one that I must create, nurture, and allow to exist and thrive inside of me; and I've learned that I can only do this, by actively seeking out and taking heed of the voice of my soul. So try not to judge me too harshly when I tell you that as I start out on this journey, it's not always easy to discern what the voice is saying; and that it seems to me, that sometimes the voice contradicts what I say I'm all about.

Shelita Peterson

The following is an excerpt from the upcoming novel *My best to be still...*

Let's not play the game

Look it doesn't matter to me! You can call me what you want! Player, hustler, gigolo, dog, bastard. Whatever! It's all good, 'cause I'm still gon' be Maurice. And the fact is, if women wouldn't play these stupid games with me I wouldn't play them either. I mean really, women are always trying to justify playing games to themselves, other women, and to men by saying that they have to, cause 'why would he buy the cow if the could get the milk for free?' Well...I say, a woman (that is, not a little girl trying to trap a man) understands the answer to that question. And it's real simple, he wouldn't buy the "cow" if the "milk" was just like "milk" he could get from any other "cow" for free. Who would? That's not intelligent! It wouldn't make sense to do that. But, if she understands and makes *him* understand that her "milk" is more tasty than anything any of those other heifers out there have to offer, then that brother would beg, borrow, steal, take out a loan, hock all of his shit, or do whatever he has to do to get the cash together to make the purchase. Now, I believe that all brothers know this at least on some level, and where females tend to get jammed up is when they aren't sure about how good their stuff is in relation to the next female. That's why all these women can write books about 'claiming your power' or what have you. *And* that's why these sisters tend to get played! Because they're running around letting these other women tell them how to play games, instead of just being honest with themselves and whoever they're dealing with, about what they like, want, need, expect and absolutely refuse to deal with or do without!

Now I'm not suggesting that they should just blurt out all this shit on the first date, but if they would set their own limits and stick to them they wouldn't have half as much bullshit in their lives. See, I've studied women, I know women. *I love women.* Especially my fine brown sisters. But I wind up running game, cause that's what they're doing. It's just that we expect different outcomes from our games. The sister's I've gone out with seem to want a provider, security, and monogamy leading up to marriage and kids and so forth. Me, I want good company, a satisfying physical relationship and some variety every now and then, which doesn't have to lead to anything in particular. But that's what happens when you play games, somebody wins, somebody loses, somebody gets what they want and somebody doesn't. And not to boast, but basically, right now I'm on top of my game.

Of course, Jacqueline is different from most other females. I mean, for the most part she knows that her "milk" is the best there is out there, but even she gets caught up in the not sticking to her limits. So, I look at it like this, I'm 29 years old and I ain't got no time for bullshit. So, if a woman is straight up with me that's how I am with her, for the most part. But if she gon' play games, I'ma play 'em too. And I'ma do my damnedest to play 'em better. Cause that's my element. I don't like coming from there, but that's what's up!!

So, like when them white chicks came out with that ol' "Rules" bullshit a few years ago, I got me a copy and started playin' by the rules too. The way I see it is this, if it's good enough for her then it's good enough for me too.

Now don't get me wrong, like I said, Jacqueline is different. I mean she's straight up with me. Well, at least most of the time, she is. I think. We met about five years ago through Darryl, a mutual friend, and we've been engaged for a little over six months. But, basically, it ain't like we're married yet. And I gotta say, I've only been doing my own thing for a little while since we've been together. Al'ight, I admit that's some bullshit. I've been doing my thing for damned near the whole time we been together. And, yes, even after we got engaged. But it's not because I just want to be a bastard. I mean, I do have feelings. It's just that I ain't trying to be forty years old and wonderin' what it would be like if I had done this one or that one. Fuck that!! I'm gettin' my swerve on before it's too late. So, if I gotta be a little doggish and cliché for the next eight months or so, then so be it. Quietly, I'm sure Jacq's getting her shit off too. And as long as I don't find out about it, its whatever! And really even if she ain't or don't want to do her thing, then she should be thankin' me for gettin' it out of my system, before we jump the broom, anyway. So, technically, if you think about it, my doing these other women now, is really gon' make me a better husband then anyway.

Ah'ight, well, maybe that parts bullshit too, but at least I can admit it. The fact is, marriage scares the shit out of me. And the bottom line is that I need to be as sure as I can be that I'm not goin' have a V8 experience on my honeymoon (like "ooops, I could've had somebody with big tits", or "ooops, I could have had somebody with a juicy ass like Janet Jackson's "). Or, even worse, after I've been married for a few years, I find out that I don't really like her as a person. So, anyway you slice it, it's about a gamble and I want to be as sure as I can.

I know I'm not painting a real pretty picture of myself here, but at least I'm honest. And plus, I mean, it's not like I'm out here banging five or six chicks at the same time like some brothers I know. And believe me, I could be. But at least I try to confine myself to only one side chick at a time. I mean, damn, a brother should get some points for that if nothing else. OK, that's bullshit too, but it's where I am right now.

I say right now, because, at the risk of sounding soft, and even though my game is on point, lately the chase hasn't really been as much fun as it used to be. And the really weird shit is that when I am with another chick, sometimes I start feeling like maybe I'm wrong or something. I have no idea what that's all about. I think this wedding shit's got me trippin'…

www.ingramcontent.com/pod-product-compliance
Lightning Source LLC
Chambersburg PA
CBHW030934090426
42737CB00007B/419